KNOWING JESUS IN THE WORLD

Praying with Teilhard de Chardin

Knowing Jesus in the World

*With a Preface by
Hans-Peter Kolvenbach SJ*

Robert Faricy, SJ
and
Lucy Rooney, SND de N

ST PAULS

ST PAULS Publishing
Morpeth Terrace, London SW1P 1EP, UK

Copyright © ST PAULS 1999

ISBN 085439 575 X

Set by TuKan, High Wycombe
Produced in the EC
Printed by Interprint Ltd., Marsa, Malta

ST PAULS is an activity of the priests and brothers of the Society of St Paul who proclaim the Gospel through the media of social communication

Contents

Preface	9
Introduction	13
Suggestions for reading and praying	33
1. The heart of Jesus	35
2. The love that God has for us in Christ	41
3. Sin and forgiveness	47
4. Creation and co-creation	53
5. The Eucharist	59
6. The cross of Jesus	63
7. The cross in my life	69
8. The cross, death and growth	75
9. Redemption and co-redemption	81
10. The Lord is risen	87
11. Jesus is Lord	93
12. Mary the Mother of Jesus	99
13. The universal Christ	107
14. Hope	113
15. The contemplation to gain love	119
Notes	127

for
Sister Mary Rooney, SND de N

Note to the Reader

This book is for prayer, to help your personal prayer, a book to pray through slowly over a period of time.

The Introduction presents a survey of the life and the spirituality of Pierre Teilhard de Chardin. You might read the Introduction now, or you might read it later, skipping to the page that comes right after the Introduction, a page of suggestions on how to use the fifteen chapters for prayer.

We hope you like the book and that it helps you to pray. Writing it helped us.

Lucy Rooney, SND de N
Robert Faricy, SJ

Preface

On 10 April 1955, Pierre Teilhard de Chardin, scientist and Catholic priest, died in New York City. The publication of the greater part of his philosophical and theological works began after his death, but even now he stands out as one of the most important, influential and controversial thinkers of this century.

Father Teilhard understood the risen Jesus Christ as the future focus of the world, the central point towards which the evolution of the universe converges, the present and coming centre of the whole cosmos. The whole universe finds its evolutionary completion in Jesus Christ.

The presence and the love of the risen Christ permeate and influence and draw towards him every person and every element of the created world. And so, in Teilhard's vision of reality, we can be united with Jesus Christ in and through the world, we can find God in all things.

But in order for Jesus to rise from the dead and to become the future focal point of the converging universe, he first had to be inoculated into the world, become a personal element in the world, a part of it. He had to be conceived and born, he had to grow in grace and age and wisdom, and he had to suffer and die on the cross.

Teilhard understands the suffering and death of Jesus Christ as redemptive, as salvific, not just in a juridical sense, but as organically necessary. In his suffering and death, Jesus bore not only the weight of our sins, but the weight of the world's progress toward the end-time when he will come again, and when this world will come to an end and be transformed into the world to come. By his cross Jesus has the victory over sin, over all that oppresses us, over death itself. The cross, much more than simply a symbol of reparation and expiation, stands for progress and victory through suffering love and difficult labour. The cross is the symbol of the synthesis of the "upward" component of sacrifice and adoring reparation, and the "forward" component of progress through laborious effort.

Jesus, then, is truly he who bears the sins of the world; moral evil is mysteriously compensated for by suffering. But more fundamentally, Jesus is he who structurally overcomes in himself, and for all of us, the resistance to spiritual ascent, a resistance inherent in matter.

For Teilhard, overcoming the world does not mean turning away from the world. Rather, overcoming the world means turning towards it in the full consciousness that with worldly effort one pursues not simply material purposes, but co-operates with God's creative and redemptive action in Jesus Christ. In this way, Teilhard, following Ignatius of Loyola, is able to find God in the world and through the world without giving himself over to some kind of pantheism. He realises that God works not only everywhere in the world, but also transcends the world and stands infinitely beyond it. God does not need the world, but we need the world in order to arrive at God.

Only a few people of his generation have held as deeply and as passionately as Teilhard the enormous hopes and the great enthusiasm of his epoch. Teilhard was not a stranger to any field of human thought or action. But he knew at the same time that the world needs Jesus Christ, and this modern world cannot be saved except through Jesus Christ. Teilhard's knowledge of the world's need for Jesus Christ rested on a living experience which he took as exemplary for others and so not just for himself.

To show the modern world that way to Jesus Christ: this was the mission that Teilhard embodied. This mission filled him with the desire to communicate the good news of Jesus to everyone whether or not it was easy to communicate, and without caution, without shirking any kind of risk. Teilhard's own passionate faith moved him towards other human beings, and his faith led him to recognise the active presence of Jesus Christ in them and in the world around them.

It is with pleasure that on the occasion of writing this preface I am able to thank God for the life and work of this companion of Jesus.

Hans-Peter Kolvenbach SJ
Superior General of the Society of Jesus
Rome, 1 January 1998

Introduction

Pierre Teilhard de Chardin: All things in Christ

Both a Roman Catholic priest and a scientist, Pierre Teilhard de Chardin lived at the intersection of two worlds, the world of religion and the world of research science. Teilhard's life as a Jesuit priest and, at the same time, scientist, can be taken as a kind of symbol of the life of most Christians today, both sacred and secular, both religious and in the world. The two components of Teilhard's life, research in science and union with God, may well represent the two components of the life of Christians today: concern with the things of this world and concern to be united with God.

In fact, he understood the integration of these two components, the "horizontal" component of involvement in the world and the "vertical" component of involvement with God, as the problem of the typical Christian today. He called it "the problem of the two faiths". How can I integrate my faith in the world and my faith in God? How can I integrate the two vectors in my life, the "forward" of life in the world and the "upward" to God?

Pierre Teilhard de Chardin not only lived that integration, but he expressed it in his religious writings, the writings that he considered to be his real life's work and his special vocation.

The solution, Teilhard wants to tell us, lies in Jesus Christ risen, the God of the Forward as well as the God of the Upward, the Lord of all things, earth as well as heaven, and in union with him in and through the world that has its existence and its meaning and its movement in Jesus Christ and through him.

At the time of Teilhard's death on Easter Sunday, 1955, he was little known outside of the Society of Jesus – the Jesuits, and the world of science. Soon after, however, the publication of his philosophical and religious works began, and volumes appeared slowly, first in French and then in other languages. In the 1960's Teilhard was intellectually fashionable partly for his broadly scientific philosophy and partly because he had been persecuted by church authorities. But, except for one important book, *The Divine Milieu*, his spiritual teaching as well as his theology of Jesus Christ remained mostly unpublished and therefore unknown until well after the Teilhard fad had passed.

In continental Europe, however, many theologians were somewhat familiar with his theological ideas from reading carbon copies of his unpublished essays, circulated among friends and gradually over the years extending to a wider circle of professional theologians. And so several of the theologians at the Second Vatican Council were strongly influenced by Teilhard.

Early years

Born in Sarcenat in central France on 1 May 1881, into a pious and prosperous Catholic family, the fourth of eleven children, Teilhard grew up in an atmosphere of traditional Catholicism and turn of the century piety. His first prayers were to the Infant Jesus, and, a little later, to the Sacred

Heart of Jesus. He never stopped praying to the heart of Jesus, and that prayer became the inspiration and the moving force in the formulation of his spiritual doctrine.

As a child, Teilhard loved objects that were hard and that seemed permanent. When his mother cut his hair and little Pierre saw the clippings, thrown in the fireplace fire, burn, he cried at the perishability. He liked iron objects, but when he found that they rusted and pitted, he changed his attachment to the quartz that lay just under a layer of soil all over the countryside.

Teilhard's childhood prayer and devotion developed over the years into a mature faith. And his love of rocks matured into a love of the science of the earth, geology. Sent for elementary and secondary school to the Jesuit boarding school at Villefranche on the Saone river, he sensed, vaguely but surely, a tension between his two loves; a tension that he would later recognise as that between two apparently diverging vectors: the "upward" towards God and the "forward" towards involvement in this world. He felt that he would have to make a choice. He did, at the end of his secondary schooling. He decided to choose "the more perfect", to "leave the world", and to enter the Jesuit novitiate at Aix-en-Provence.

The novitiate turned out to be difficult for Teilhard, he often felt homesick. But he took perpetual vows along with the others in his novitiate class in 1901.

Jesuit formation

At the beginning of the twentieth century, the French government, even down to the local offices, was strongly anti-Catholic. In 1901 anti-clerical laws were passed in France, Jesuit students were sent abroad for studies, since it was impossible for them to study in France. And so, after the novitiate, the order sent Teilhard along with his vow class to study science, humanities, and philosophy for four years on the British island of Jersey, just off the northern French coast. He found himself especially at home in the science courses, and above all with physics. Encouraged by his superiors, he found himself returning to his love of the "science of rocks". And he felt the tension again between his scientific tendencies and his love of the earth. He sought counsel from his former novice master, who – without resolving the problem wisely but somewhat vaguely directed him to give himself fully to both tendencies, that the development of his natural talents and interests was according to the will of God, and that things would work out. Eventually they did. Teilhard never again found himself tempted to go only in one of the two directions. And his life began to be more integrated.

Teilhard de Chardin continued to follow the traditional Jesuit programme of formation. After the novitiate and after studies in the humanities, sciences, and in philosophy, he taught for three years: chemistry and physics in the Jesuit secondary school in Cairo, Egypt. In his spare time and during vacations, he pursued his interest in "the earth" and developed a certain competence in field research.

After Cairo, the Jesuit order sent Teilhard to study theology for four years from 1908 to 1912, at Hastings in the south of England, where the French Jesuits had established a French-speaking theology school. Here too, he used much of his spare time searching for fossilised forms of life. Ordained a priest in 1911, he finished his theological studies at Hastings and then was sent to Paris to live in a small Jesuit community there and to study geology at the Catholic Institute and to study palaeontology, the science of fossils, at the Paris Museum of Natural History under Marcel Boule, at that time one of the world's best known palaeontologists.

The First World War

In early August, 1914, Germany declared war on France, invaded Belgium and then France, and marched towards Paris. Drafted into the army as a stretcher bearer in 1914, Teilhard interrupted his studies and spent the First World War mostly in combat, carrying a stretcher and later as chaplain without army rank, in a regiment composed of Frenchmen and Moslem North Africans from French colonies. Before the war ended, Teilhard had been cited in dispatches on several occasions. The citations noted that: he "volunteered to leave the aid post in order to serve in the front line trenches, and displayed the greatest self-sacrifice and contempt for danger" (1915). "A model of bravery, self-sacrifice, and coolness. From 15th to 19th August he directed the teams of stretcher bearers over ground torn by shell-fire and swept by machine guns. On 18th he went out to within twenty yards of the enemy lines to retrieve the body of a fallen officer and brought it back to the trenches" (1916). In June 1917 Teilhard was awarded the *Medaille Militaire* as "A first-rate N.C.O. whose sterling character has won him confidence and respect. On 20th May he deliberately entered a trench under heavy bombardment to bring back a casualty." After the war was over, at the request of his old regiment he was made a Chevalier of the Legion of Honour. The citation described Teilhard as "An outstanding stretcher-bearer, who during four years of active service, was in every battle and engagement the regiment took part in, applying to remain in the ranks in order that he might be with the men, whose dangers and hardships he constantly shared."

In 1916, during a rest from action at the front, behind the lines, Teilhard began to take notes, writing his reflections in a notebook and then organising and expanding those ideas into about twenty essays.

Although Teilhard had already published some theological articles, they were in a classical mould. His original thinking began at the front during the war. The centre and heart of that thinking was the apparent conflict between the "two absolutes", God and the world, and the resolution of that seeming conflict in the person of Jesus Christ risen, God in human form in whom the world is rooted and towards whom it is going.

From now on the idea of evolution formed the framework of Teilhard's thought. He wanted to rethink the theology of Jesus Christ and his relationship with the world according to the content of the Pauline epistles and in the category of the modern idea of evolution. An integrated understanding of Jesus Christ and the world would form the foundation for an understanding of how prayer and action could be integrated, how our "forward" impulse towards involvement in the world and its progress could come together with our "upward" impulse towards God.

From Paris to China

After the war, Teilhard, discharged from the army, made a brief visit to his family and then returned to Paris to continue his studies. Even before he had finished his doctoral thesis he began to teach palaeontology at the Catholic Institute, and two years later, completed his doctorate work. From now on, he was a fully trained, full-time, dedicated scientist with a speciality of dating rocks by means of the fossils found in them. This, of course, demanded field research, long trips, digging for fossils, and examining them and classifying them. He also researched early human artefacts, especially flints that had been formed into tools. He had a sharp eye, could spot things others missed, and rarely forgot the details of anything he had been involved in finding. In fact, he discovered fossils of plants and animals previously unknown, among them, in 1927 in Belgium, a fossil of the most primitive of the then known primates, an entirely new genus now named in his honour, *Teilhardina*.

His lectures at the Catholic Institute in Paris were well attended, and Teilhard attracted a considerable following in Paris. Catholic students of science, especially those who felt torn between their belief in evolution and their faith, listened carefully to Teilhard, and found peace in what he taught.

Teilhard asked for a leave of absence for the academic year 1923-1924, and spent it in Tientsin, China, where a French scientist wanted to set up a scientific museum and had asked for Teilhard's help. He returned to Paris, now forty three years old, in the autumn of 1924 and began teaching again. Conservative Catholics in the Paris university milieu resented the influence Teilhard and his ideas had on Catholic graduate students not only at the Catholic Institute but at the other graduate schools in Paris. They obtained copies of some of his more spiritual and theological talks and essays, and sent them to the Jesuit headquarters in Rome, and to the Vatican. The Vatican file on Teilhard began to grow.

In particular, an outline for a talk on original sin, sketching out ways that the dogma could be interpreted in an evolutionary framework, was taken by an unknown person from a desk drawer in Teilhard's bedroom and mailed with comments to the Jesuit General in Rome. The result: in April, 1926, Teilhard's Jesuit order sent him to China to work there. Exiled by church superiors from Europe, and in particular from Paris, he would be based in China for nearly twenty years, working as a geologist and palaeontologist.

In China, Teilhard became a founder of the science of geology there, doing basic research work, travelling all over China, publishing articles in international scientific journals, attending scientific conventions, often in Europe or the United States, going on expedition not only in China but even in Africa, India, and Java. By 1940, he had an excellent international reputation as a scientist. In 1929, as adviser to the Geological Survey of China, he shared in the discovery, and the subsequent study, of Peking Man, the fossil man, *Sinanthropus*.

His priestly work was almost non-existent. In Beijing, where Teilhard lived after 1929, only priest members of the Vincentian order were allowed to preach and hear confessions. Jesuits could not do any pastoral ministry there. Teilhard said his daily Mass, at least when he was not on expedition and could not, made his daily meditation and examinations of conscience, prayed his breviary, grew in union with the Lord. But he was rarely allowed to act as a priest in the way that he had in Paris.

Teilhard and his philosophical and religious ideas remained a problem in the Catholic Church and especially in his own religious order. In 1937, he travelled to the east coast of the United States to receive the Gregor Mendel medal from Villanova University in Philadelphia and an honorary doctorate from the Jesuit-run Boston College. But after his acceptance talk at Villanova, not just a few words but an intellectual talk on the importance of evolution, Boston College decided not to give Teilhard the honorary doctorate after all. The idea of evolution was not accepted in Catholic America.

Teilhard grew more frustrated every year at his failure to obtain superiors' permission to publish his religious, theological, and spiritual writings. The essays and books kept piling up in his room, sometimes sent to friends in Europe and there re-typed with carbon copies and sent to others. But never published. Teilhard finished his spiritual classic, *The Divine Milieu*, in 1926, and sent copies of it to friends for comments. The Jesuit censors turned it down. In 1944, he sent a copy of *The Phenomenon of Man* to Jesuit headquarters in Rome asking permission to publish it. They refused the necessary approval. Teilhard kept writing.

In 1938, Jeanne Mortier, an unmarried Parisian, offered to be of help to Teilhard. He asked her to establish a kind of depot for his unpublished writings in Paris. She did, and from then on, his religious writings went out from Miss Mortier to a network of Teilhard's friends in Europe and especially in France.

Teilhard stayed in Beijing during World War II. In May 1946, he left China and went home to France.

The last decade

Welcomed in Paris as an eminent scientist, elected in 1950 to the Academy of Sciences, decorated for scientific achievement by the French government, appointed to several prestigious scientific academies and societies, Teilhard found French Catholic intellectual life considerably changed. The conservatives had supported the Nazi-sponsored government of General Petain in France, and now were quite out of favour. People with more progressive ideas, many of whom had fought in the French resistance, gave new life to the French Catholic Church. It was the time of priest-workers, of liturgical innovations, and of the "new theology" of Henri de Lubac, Jean Danielou, and others, many of them Jesuits. And Teilhard found his family and old friends, and made new friends in both France and Great Britain, like Julian Huxley. In February of 1949, the new Jesuit General, who esteemed Teilhard and who liked him, nevertheless informed Teilhard that, once again, his writings had not passed the censors, and that in particular his three complete books, *The Divine Milieu*, *The Phenomenon of Man*, and a much better thorough revision of *The Phenomenon of Man*, called *Man's Place in Nature*, could not be published. In 1949, the conservative forces in the Church, especially in Rome, had rallied. Pope Pius XII, now elderly, had serious suspicions about French theology. Five French Jesuits, including the great Henri de Lubac, were suspended from teaching theology, Pius XII issued the encyclical *Humani Generis* condemning several deviant tendencies, including some ideas generally attributed to Teilhard, and Teilhard's superiors decided once again on his exile. This time, he went to New York City.

But before he left, Teilhard consulted a Jesuit canon lawyer and learned from him that canonists hold two views, both acceptable, on whether a member of a religious order, with a vow of poverty, could make a disposition of his writings to take place after his death. The canon lawyer advised Teilhard to follow the more favourable (to him) interpretation, and to make a will leaving all his writings to a person outside the order who would see to their publication after his death. Jesuits have a vow of poverty, and cannot personally receive or give material gifts. But they can give ideas and, some canon lawyers hold, unpublished manuscripts. Teilhard assembled all he had ever written of a philosophical or religious nature and left the manuscripts with Jeanne Mortier in Paris. And he wrote a will, leaving them all to her for what he hoped would be eventual publication.

In New York, Teilhard was given a room in the Jesuit community of about sixty priests and a few brothers at Saint Ignatius Loyola parish on Park Avenue. The Jesuits there, after a cordial and hearty welcome, left him alone; he remained a vaguely disturbing foreign presence of confusing reputation, largely ignored. He worked at the Wenner-Gren Foundation, an anthropological institute that funded scientific expeditions and publications.

In the winter of 1953-1954, now seventy two years old, Teilhard experienced another of his occasional bouts of depression. This time it was severe, made worse by a bad heart condition. He felt rejected by his Church, by the Jesuits, a total failure with all his unpublished writings, and now too old to do anything about it. He spent considerable time in bed, and took some medication.

He got better, kept working and kept writing. Then, 10 April, Easter Day, 1955, he died. Only a few people attended his funeral, and fewer still his burial at the Jesuit novitiate north of New York City. He would be better known after his death, in just a few years.

Post mortem

Jeanne Mortier began right away with the publication of *The Phenomenon of Man*. The Teilhard boom began with its translation into English in 1959, with a preface by Julian Huxley. Other writings followed: books of essays, *The Divine Milieu*, volumes of Teilhard's letters.

His writings are still appearing: collections of letters, especially. His essays and books have now all been published in French and translated into all the major languages.

Teilhard's ideas met strong opposition, especially after some of his writings had been published. There were personal attacks. It was alleged that he had serious romantic affairs with various women. It was said that he had gone against canon law by leaving his writings to Jeanne Mortier to be published. Some said that he had died outside the Jesuit order, or outside membership in a Jesuit community, or at least not in good standing in the order. He was accused of personal responsibility for a famous hoax in physical anthropology, the discovery of the Piltdown Man in England, later proved to have been faked. None of these accusations ever had any basis in fact.

And there were refutations of his ideas by respected Catholic thinkers like Jacques Maritain, Etienne Gilson, and Dietrich von Hildebrand, as well as vitriolic attacks by right wing Catholics who felt that the Second Vatican Council marked the end of real Catholicism and that Teilhard had been its false prophet. Today, however, the orthodoxy of Teilhard's thinking, and the validity of the general lines of his thought, is no longer questioned by reputable theologians, and one must listen carefully to hear the occasional reactionary murmurings against his ideas.

At the very time that the Second Vatican Council was approaching, in which Teilhard's thought would have so much influence on the debates and the documents, the Vatican itself, in 1962, published an official *monitum* regarding the works of Pierre Teilhard de Chardin. A *monitum* is a warning. In this case, Catholics were warned that his works contained ambiguities and even errors, and that they posed a danger to the orthodoxy of readers. The warning put Teilhard's writings under a cloud.

But the sky cleared once the Council began. Soon after the end of the Council, the Jesuit General, Pedro Arrupe, publicly praised Teilhard and his writings. And later, in May of 1981, Cardinal Casaroli, the Vatican Secretary of State, on behalf of Pope John Paul II, in an official letter to the Catholic Institute in Paris where celebrations marking the centenary of Teilhard's birth were taking place, spoke favourably of Teilhard de Chardin and of his thought. Teilhard, the cardinal testified, is "the witness of the unified life of a man seized by Christ in the depths of his being". Anticipating Pope John Paul II's call to bring Christ into contemporary life in all its aspects, Teilhard "responded in advance, as it were".

Teilhard was present in spirit in the discussions at the Second Vatican Council. His influence, through what had been published up to that time, and through carbon copies of his essays circulated among theologians particularly in northern Europe, was immense. Much of what is now generally seen as the most important Vatican II document, *The Pastoral Constitution on the Church in the Modern World*, reads as though Teilhard had written it himself.

Teilhard's influence on theology, especially on Christology, the theology of original sin and redemption, has been strong since the Council. Theologians like Piet Schoonenberg, Henri de Lubac, and Gustav Martelet, mined Teilhard's thought and developed it. His influence on the thought of many other theologians was great, even though not always acknowledged.

In 1965 the first doctoral thesis on Teilhard's religious

thought was defended in Paris by Christopher Mooney, a New England Jesuit, and published in both French and English. Other doctoral theses and books about Teilhard and his ideas came and continue to come, in many languages.

A fascinating figure, the image of Teilhard found its way into novels and films; he was the model for a character in Morris West's novel, *The Shoes of the Fisherman*, the model for the priest-exorcist in Peter Blatty's novel and in the film *The Exorcist*. He influenced Graham Greene, Flannery O'Connor, Thomas Merton, and others. He has been read and re-read by people as diverse as Mario Cuomo, U Thant, and President Mitterand of France.

Pierre Teilhard de Chardin is a hard man to classify, he fits into too many categories, many of them in apparent opposition. History has a hard time knowing how to describe him. Scientist and poet, an original, but scrupulously obedient, critical of some church men but a lover of all things Roman Catholic beginning with the Church herself, a man of deep prayer and a man of action, alone and lonely but a man who attracted friendship, cheerful and peaceful but sometimes deeply depressed or agitated, Teilhard was a man of too many parts to fit neatly into a classification system. His spirituality, too, is a combination of many things, expressed in poetic language, in mystical language, in the language of science, and sometimes in words and phrases he invented himself.

He was as complicated and as made up of contradictory elements as most of us are, and he needed many kinds of language to express a spirituality for our times.

Teilhard's spirituality

It is in the area of spirituality that Teilhard's influence has been the greatest. Today, most of his writings have been published. And Christians recognise that his real importance for us lies in his spirituality of Christian life, a life centred on Jesus risen in the world, a world centred on that same risen Christ. Teilhard helps us to come closer to the Lord. He helps us to pray.

The spirituality of Pierre Teilhard de Chardin finds its foundations in his Christology, in his theology of Jesus Christ and the world's relation to him. And Teilhard's Christology is rooted in two sources: Scripture as interpreted by Tradition, and Teilhard's own theory of evolution. Every Christian theologian works from two sources: Scripture as interpreted by Tradition, and some framework of interpretation. Saint Thomas Aquinas used Scripture and, as a framework of interpretation of the data of Scripture, his own version of Aristotle's philosophy. Karl Rahner used for his two sources: Scripture and his particular brand of Thomist philosophy together with the philosophies of Martin Heidegger and Edmund Husserl.

Teilhard's sources are scripture and, as his framework within which to interpret Scripture for our times, his own theory of evolution. In Teilhard's idea of evolution, evolution converges towards a future focal point. Since the time that human beings appeared in evolutionary process, the form that evolution takes is human progress, and – in human progress – evolution converges towards a point in the future. Think of a cone lying on its side. The tip of the cone is the Second Coming of Christ; the bottom section of the cone is the past. We are somewhere in the cone, moving towards the apex.

In his Christology, Teilhard identifies that future focal point, the apex of the cone of time, with the Second Coming of Christ. But he understands it not so much as Jesus coming a second time as the world finally reaching him.

Teilhard's spirituality is built on his theology of Jesus Christ. What are the main themes of that spirituality?

Personal relationship with Jesus Christ: The centre and axis of Teilhard's spirituality is personal relationship with Jesus Christ risen, a relationship in and through the world.

Continuous creation: Teilhard understands creation not so much as a divine act in the beginning as a now ongoing process. Jesus, the focal centre of all history, the world's and mine, draws all things to himself, holding them in existence through his universal love. This process is creation: Jesus drawing the world to himself, reconciling all things in himself in whom everything holds together.

Co-creation: *Whatever we do in the direction of unification, of love, of building or maintaining towards Jesus, towards the Kingdom, participates in the process of creation, of the reconciliation of all things in Jesus.* We are co-creators with the Creator.

And so what I do or undergo has value, not just for this world but for the world to come, and not just because I offer it to the Lord or have a right intention in doing or undergoing it. *What I do and what I undergo is important in itself; does something, builds, prepares for the time when this world will end and be transformed.*

The Eucharist: *Jesus risen in the Eucharist is the same Jesus in whom the world holds together and towards whom it moves.* Therefore the Eucharist has a universal and even cosmic significance and importance. All the Masses of history form a line that is the central axis of history and of all true progress moving towards its focal point.

The cross in Jesus' life and in mine: *The cross in Teilhard's spirituality is not just the symbol of expiation and reparation for sin, but the positive symbol and the real act, of difficult labour and of undergoing suffering, of Jesus raising up the world.* My own suffering, whether active – due to necessary discipline, or hard work, or positive sacrifice; or passive-suffering undergone from what I cannot change or avoid: illness, failure, rejections, death; my suffering shares in the cross of Jesus, shares in his redemptive work, makes up what has been wanting in his sufferings. I can carry my cross knowing that what I do has real redemptive value, shares positively and actively in the redemption, in the process of redemption that Jesus made possible and began by his suffering and death on the cross.

Death and the paschal mystery: The greatest cross and the last enemy, death, preoccupied Teilhard in his later years. He writes about it not only in essays and books, but in his personal spiritual notes. *Death is not the end, but a passage to full union with Jesus.*

The paschal mystery: The mystery of the death and resurrection of Jesus, stands as the paradigm of the process of Christian existence: life and growth, death, resurrection. Growth and building, destruction and fragmentation, re-centring and re-integration in a new synthesis. My life, death, re-integration after death in a new centring on Jesus in the life to come, is my participation in the paschal mystery, in the mystery of the life, death, resurrection of Jesus Christ. *I live that paschal mystery every day*, building up provisory unities, undergoing their fragmentations and undoings – carrying those crosses in union with Jesus, and letting the Lord put me together again in a new synthesis, this time more centred on him and less centred on myself.

The Second Coming of Christ: The Parousia, the Second Coming of Jesus, is the central mystery of Teilhard's theology and spirituality. Every theologian works from a central Christian mystery. Thomas Aquinas and Karl Rahner: the Incarnation; Wolfhart Pannenberg: the Resurrection; Martin Luther and many Lutheran theologians: the Cross. Pierre Teilhard de Chardin: the Parousia. He understands all reality in faith in the light of Jesus coming at the end of the world, or – rather – the world reaching Jesus who draws it to himself.

Love: In Teilhard's spirituality, love has the primacy, love does everything. Love unites, not surface to surface but heart to heart, and therefore freely and strongly. Love creates. Love saves. Love redeems. Love is the glue that holds everything together. Love holds primacy: God's love for each of us and for the world in Jesus, the love of Jesus for each of us and for the world, our love for one another.

The heart of Jesus: The heart of Jesus is less a major theme of Teilhard's writings than of his personal, and mostly unpublished, spiritual notes, including the notes he took during his annual re treats. Jesus is the heart of the world. And his heart *is the heart of the heart of the world.*

The idea of Jesus' heart in Teilhard's spirituality brings out the fact that Jesus' love, including his mercy and his forgiveness, is his main quality and his main activity. Furthermore, the idea of "heart" connotes the idea of "core", "centre". For Teilhard, the risen Jesus is the core and the personal centre of the universe.

Teilhard for today

Teilhard is a teacher for our times. He shows us the Christ of the Bible, the Jesus of the Gospels, of the Pauline letters, and of the Apocalypse, in the framework of a contemporary worldview and of contemporary experience. He teaches us where to look for Jesus and how to find him.

Teilhard de Chardin helps us to pray, and to integrate our prayer and the rest of our lives. He helps us to live in the world, in union with Jesus who is the Heart of the world. Teilhard helps us to love with the knowledge and appreciation of the fact that Jesus loves us first and most, that he loves whom and what we love, and that he helps us to love as we should.

Suggestions for reading and praying

Each of the fifteen chapters begins with a grace to ask for and with a brief prayer. We suggest that you ask the Lord for this grace, this special gift, for the time that you remain with that particular chapter. And that you make the short prayer your own.

There follow a few pages of reading about the life and the spirituality of Pierre Teilhard de Chardin. After these pages come some "Prayerful Considerations". The considerations are for prayer.

Suggestion: read the "Prayerful Considerations" one at a time, and slowly. Stop as soon as something – a word, a phrase, an idea – speaks to your heart. Pray about it; turn to the Lord and be with him about what you have just read. Stay there until you feel it is time to move on. Then go to the next consideration.

The Scripture text, entitled "God's Word", comes next, after the considerations. The Scripture has been selected for prayer, to lead to prayer. You might read it prayerfully, stopping to relate to the Lord in terms of each phrase or concept in the text.

Finally, the "Closing Prayer" can be used in two ways: you could read it, use it, to end your prayer time. Or you could make it the principal part of your prayer. In this case, you might read it as slowly as possible. After the first few words of the prayer, turn right to the Lord and just stay there in silence. To help to remain with the Lord in silence, you could repeat over and over, just as slowly as you can, and meaning what you pray, a word or a few words from the prayer. Stay with Jesus, contemplating him in the context of the words from the prayer, as long as you are at all comfortable with him and with what you are doing.

1

The heart of Jesus

The grace I ask: To *know* that Jesus has a personal love for me in his heart, the heart that is the centre of the world.

Prayer: Lord Jesus, I ask the grace from you to understand better your personal love of me, that you call me by name, know me perfectly. Without any qualifications you love me just as I am now. Help me to enter into your love of me.

Teilhard

From his earliest childhood, Teilhard knew and had devotion to the heart of Jesus Christ. In adulthood, his explicit love for the heart of Jesus animated his philosophical and religious thinking and writing. As a result, all his writings have as their almost invisible foundation the heart of Christ.

The God that Teilhard's mother taught him to revere in his childhood was an incarnate God, Jesus, the Word made flesh, the Sacred Heart. In the Sacred Heart Teilhard found a centre for his world. He found God's love universalised and humanised in the heart of Jesus, and he found the world personalised because centred on the heart of the centre of the world, Jesus Christ. In his devotion to the Lord's heart, Teilhard's love for life and his yearning for God came together.

Even before he became a priest Teilhard's attachment to the heart of Jesus had begun to synthesise his "upward" impulse towards God and his "forward" impulse to involvement in the world around him. He was both a Christian and a lover of the world, both a priest and a scientist, a man of God and a man of his time. On the Isle of Jersey, at the beginning of his Jesuit studies, Teilhard had already begun to study geology with great enthusiasm. He realised that his love for what he called "the study of rocks" was just one expression of his love of life and of the world. This reflection precipitated a real crisis in his life and in his Jesuit vocation. How could he avoid being torn between his drive upward towards God and his drive forward towards the world, between his priesthood and his scientific research, between his faith in God and his faith in the world? Teilhard went to his spiritual father, until recently his novice master for two years, for advice on how to reconcile his love of life and especially of geological research, and his love of the Lord. The advice the novice master gave Teilhard: to love both with all his heart, and the two loves would come together. "What he said," Teilhard wrote many years later, "was enough to leave me with a firm grasp of both ends of the line."[1]

Only in a unified understanding of Jesus who both loved him, Teilhard, personally and who at the same time centred the world, Teilhard's world and the whole world, on himself could Teilhard find peace and room to grow. The negative aspects of much traditional devotion to the Sacred Heart never hemmed Teilhard in. He found the traditional devotion limited, narrow. In his retreat of 1939 he writes *"The Sacred Heart:* Instinctively and mysteriously since my infancy: the *synthesis* of love and matter, of person and energy... I would like to spread, effectively, the attraction (I do not want to say the word 'devotion', much too sentimental and too weak) to the universal Christ, to the *true* heart of Jesus." The Sacred Heart that Teilhard knew was big enough to embrace the whole world and human and personal enough to know him, Teilhard, personally, to call him by name, to love him totally and unqualifiedly.

A reading from Teilhard

> I have never had at any point in my life the slightest difficulty in addressing God as a supreme SOMEONE,... centre to centre, heart to heart... Going in this direction was made easier by the fact that my mother's God was above all, for me as well as for her, the *incarnate* Word. This was enough to establish from the beginning a primary contact, through the humanity of Jesus, between the two halves of the core of my being, the "Christian" and the "pagan"... It would be difficult for me to make anyone understand how deeply, vigorously and constantly... my religious life in the pre-war years developed under the sign of and in wonderment at the heart of Jesus. *("Le coeur de la matière,"* in *Le coeur de la matière,* Seuil, 1976, pages 52-54.)

Prayerful considerations

Read the following considerations if they are helpful, but stop at any point where you turn to the heart of Jesus in prayer. Teilhard writes: "Jesus only, only Jesus. His holy presence ought gradually to absorb me."

From the heart of the risen Jesus, present to me now, come streams of love that go out to everything and to everyone, and to each person personally and in an individualised way. Jesus' love for me has my name on it. How does Jesus love me?

Consider the teaching of Jesus in the Gospel of Luke, chapter 6, verses 36 to 38: "Be compassionate just as your Father is compassionate. Do not judge, and you will not be judged; do not condemn, and you will not be condemned. Give, and there will be gifts for you." You know that Jesus practises what he preaches. So turn this teaching around and apply it to *his* love for you. Jesus does not judge me, and so on.

Look at Paul's description of love in the First Letter to the Corinthians, chapter 13, verses 4 to 7: "Love is always patient and kind; love is never jealous; love is not boastful or conceited; love is never rude; and love never seeks its own advantage, love does not take offence or store up grievances. Love does not rejoice in wrong doing, but finds its joy in the truth. Love is always ready to make allowances, to trust, to hope, and to endure whatever comes." God is love; we know that from John's Gospel. And we know from Christian teaching that Jesus is God. If Jesus is God, and God is love, then Jesus is love. This is a theologically accurate statement. So go through the above scripture passage slowly, this time substituting the word "Jesus" for the word "love".

What will that give you? A personality profile of

Jesus insofar as he loves you, the quality of his love for you, how he loves you. Then stay with the text awhile, resting in the Lord's love or talking to him about it, or thanking him for loving you.

- Consider the things that you do not like about yourself: your sins, your bad habits, your limitations, maybe your looks. Then consider that Jesus is not you, that he does not share your way of looking at yourself. He has compassion towards you, and your sins and weaknesses are the opening in you for his compassion and love, part of what makes you attractive to him. He finds you wonderful, beautiful. He loves you. Thank him for that.

- Read the Scripture text below, from John's Gospel, under the title "God's Word", slowly and thoughtfully, pausing after each phrase. Then leave the text and stay in the presence of Jesus quietly, talking to him or asking him about the text, or just relating to him in silence, or repeating a short prayer over and over, like "Thank you Jesus, for loving me."

- Often during the day repeat the short prayer, "Thank you, Jesus, for loving me."

God's Word

Jesus stood and cried out:
'Let anyone who is thirsty come to me!
Let anyone who believes in me
come and drink!
As scripture says, "From his heart shall flow streams of living water"' (Jn 7:37-38).

Closing prayer: "Lord, close me up inside the deepest part of your heart; and, holding me there, burn me, set me on fire, purify me…" (Teilhard, *Hymne de l'univers,* Seuil, 1961, page 32).

2

The love that God has for us in Christ

The grace I ask: The conviction that the risen Jesus, true God and truly human, loves me personally just as I am.

Prayer: Lord Jesus, help me to know you better as loving me. Help me to enter into your love of me.

Teilhard

After finishing his Jesuit studies in philosophy and theology, and after having taught for three years in a Jesuit secondary school in Cairo, and after having been ordained a priest, Teilhard found himself drafted into the French army at the beginning of the First World War in 1914. Assigned to a regiment of North African Zouaves, a unit especially active in fighting against the German army that had invaded Belgium, Teilhard lived through bullets and poison gas that took more than half the men in his regiment. His affection and admiration for these men is evident in Teilhard's letters from the front to his cousin Marguerite: "I forgot to tell you that here I am with *real* and excellent officers. It can't but hearten one to work with such M.O.s as these." He wrote to ask Marguerite to send a football for the men, and adds: "I feel increasingly happy at having been posted to a regiment in which I am the only priest, and where there is a large number of men who, when the time comes, will turn to me for help." He continues: "Thanks to the powerful voices of the Bordelais, of whom there are many in my section, our evening Benediction is quite impressive. At the moment, a little talent for music or cooking would serve me better than all my palaeontology." Receiving one of Marguerite's relief parcels, he writes: "The 2nd Moroccan ambulance has just gleefully shared the contents of the parcel so generously sent... I kept in particular for myself the friendship with which, at least as much as with woollen comforts, it was filled."[2]

According to his conscience and the rules of the Catholic Church in France, he served first as a stretcher bearer, not as a combatant. Of course, he continued to pray regularly, meditating at least an hour a day, to say Mass every day at least when that was possible, and to pray the Divine Office from the breviary as every Catholic priest does.

While serving at the front, amid the horrors of the war, Teilhard had some properly mystical experiences of Christ, probably beginning around March or April, 1916. He understood, or rather experienced, the presence of the risen Jesus Christ in the world through his love, an intimate presence-through-love in the whole of creation. These experiences showed him the mystery of God's presence through Jesus Christ in the world, and they changed Teilhard forever. From then on, he had a new vision of reality, he saw things differently.

God was not "up there", above, in some way distant.

He was here, in Jesus risen, through the intense love that radiates out from the heart of Jesus, present to everything created, and to all of creation together, and to Teilhard, through the love of the risen Christ for each creature and for all creation. Teilhard described these experiences later in an essay, attributing the visions to a fictitious person, and writing about them as fiction.[3] We know, however, from conversations with Jeanne Mortier, Teilhard's secretary for many years, that – far from made up – the experiences happened to Teilhard himself.

He kept notes on these experiences, and on his reflections on them, in small notebooks, the kind that French school children still use. These notes, in turn, became the basis of essays, the first descriptions of Teilhard's Christian understanding of reality and of his spirituality. He began to write his reflections on these experiences, in the form of notes and then essays, in the spring of 1916. At Verdun, east of the Meuse river, between Rheims and Metz, Teilhard recorded his mystical experiences, as fiction, in the form of three stories. The following comes from the first story, called "The Picture."

A reading from Teilhard

> My mind was occupied with a problem that was part philosophical and part aesthetic. I thought: suppose Christ should choose to appear bodily here before me, what would he look like? How would he be dressed? Above all, how would he become material, and in what way would he stand out against the objects surrounding him?... Meanwhile, my gaze fastened itself without any thought on my part on a picture of Christ offering his heart to us. This picture hung in front of me on the wall of a church into which I had gone to pray... My

vision began. To tell the truth, I could not say exactly when it began, for it already had a certain intensity when I became conscious of it. As I allowed my gaze to wander over the picture I suddenly became aware that the picture was *melting;* it was melting in a special manner, hard to describe... The vibrant atmosphere which surrounded Christ like an aureole was no longer confined to a small space around him, but radiated outward to infinity... *The entire universe was vibrant!* And yet, when I looked at particular objects, one by one, I found them still as clearly delineated as ever and preserved in their individuality.

All this movement seemed to emanate from Christ, above all from his heart... And I stood dumbfounded... When I was able to look at it again, the picture of Christ in the church had once again taken on its fixed features. *(Hymne de l'universe,* op.sit. pages 42-46.)

Prayerful considerations

In the notes he kept of his 1948 retreat, Teilhard has only four words to record on the seventh day of his eight day retreat. He writes: "Re-meditate the Golden Glow." (The words "the Golden Glow" are in English). "The Golden Glow" appears in only one other place in Teilhard's writings, on a 'holy card' of the Sacred Heart, found after his death, among the things on his desk. On the front of the picture is written "Jesus, the Heart of the World". On the back is a litany, a series of titles or appellations for the Sacred Heart... The last is "The Golden Glow".

Teilhard de Chardin's vision of Jesus risen who fills the whole world with his love, while a vision, represents a truth. Jesus' love *does* fill the world. And yet, he does not love all things indistinctly, all grouped and merged together. He loves each thing, and in particular each person, individually. The vision of Teilhard was a vision; but the love of Jesus is real, then and now, for him and for you.

- Jesus loves you, all the people in your life, and the world around you. Because it all holds together in him. Read the beginning of the prologue to John's Gospel, chapter 1, verses 1 to 5: "In the beginning was the Word:... through him all things came into being... And light shines in darkness." The love of Jesus, for you and for all, shines in the darkness around you.

- Read, too, Paul's Letter to the Colossians, chapter 1, verses 15 to 20. "In him all things hold together." You hold together in Jesus, in his love. And so does everyone around you. And the world around you.

- Look up and understand, seeing with the eyes of faith, that the love of Jesus fills the place where you are. That *you are* in his love. That it fills you, and it fills your world. And that his love for you is personal, not merging you with everyone and everything else, but singling you out, reaching you as a person in your own particularity and in your own individuality.

- Often during the day repeat the short prayer, "Thank you, Jesus, for loving the world, and for loving me personally just as I am."

- Read the Scripture text in the next paragraph, "God's Word." Pray it, saying the words of the Psalm to Jesus as slowly as you comfortably can. Then put the text aside and be with Jesus present and loving you. Speak to him in your own words. Ask him questions. Or just be quiet in his presence.

Keep the text at hand in case you have distractions; you can always go back to the text and it will turn you to Jesus.

God's Word

Lord, you search me and know me.
You know if I am standing or sitting.
You perceive my thoughts from far away.
Whether I walk or lie down, you are watching;
you are familiar with all my ways.
Before a word is even on my tongue, Lord,
you know it completely.
Close behind and close in front you hem me in,
shielding me with your hand.
Such knowledge is beyond my understanding,
too high beyond my reach.
Where could I go to escape your spirit?
Where could I flee from your presence?
If I climb to the heavens, you are there;
there too if I sink to Sheol.
If I flew to the point of sunrise –
or far across the sea –
your hand would still be guiding me,
your right hand holding me.
If I asked darkness to cover me
and light to become night around me,
that darkness would not be dark to you;
night would shine as the day.
(Ps 139:1-12)

Closing prayer: "Lord, close me up in the deepest recesses of your heart." (Teilhard wrote this prayer in Latin: *"Tu autem, Domine mi, include me in imis visceribus Cordis tui." Hymne de l'univers,* op.sit. page 32.)

3

Sin and forgiveness

The grace I ask: Jesus reveal to me my sinfulness, and then forgive me.

Prayer: Lord Jesus, shine the light of your love on me, reveal to me my sins, and my sinfulness, in the light of your personal love for me. Give me the grace to be sorry, and the grace to accept fully your merciful forgiveness.

Teilhard

Pierre Teilhard de Chardin knew suffering, death, sin, and all the kinds of evil in the world. Having volunteered for service where the fighting was worst, decorated twice for outstanding bravery, Teilhard experienced at first hand and up close perhaps the most ghastly and gruesome of all the world's wars. And he knew misunderstanding and rejection at the hands of his friends and of his own religious community, the Society of Jesus. Besides that, he carried all his life a severe anxiety that in later life became even more acute because of a serious heart condition.

That anxiety gave him trouble in 1916 and in 1917;

he saw just too much suffering and ugly death. His brother Olivier, an officer on the northern front, died there in early May; his brother Gonzague had already been killed early in the war. Teilhard's earliest essays, sent to his Jesuit superiors, provoked opposition to Teilhard and great concern about his orthodoxy. His superiors seriously considered not admitting him to final and solemn vows in the Society of Jesus.

In the spring of 1917, Teilhard, reflecting on sin, suffering, and death in the world, first sketched out his own understanding of what sin means, of what suffering is, of the meaning of death. He put his ideas together in an essay entitled, "The Struggle against the Multitude." He understands evil in the world at every level as a product of a multiplicity that continually strives toward a unity. The world moves forward in evolution, toward a goal that, ultimately, faith tells us, consists in the Second Coming of the risen Christ, the end of this world, and the beginning of the world to come when God will be all in all. The world evolves, then, always in the general direction of the final unification of all things in Christ, striving to make a unity out of its own multiplicity.

What is the result? Breakage, waste, and failure, and at every level. Evil exists with a certain statistical inevitability in a multiplicity moving toward a unity. There is no other path to unity except through a certain amount of breakage, waste, failure. At the biological level, this means suffering and death. At the moral level, it means sin. Sin is inevitable. We are free, and so we are free to sin. And so, inevitably, we do, not necessarily in any given case, but inevitably in some cases. We are all sinners. No exceptions. As a Jesuit novice, and then a scholastic, and finally as a Jesuit priest, Teilhard made a silent retreat, lasting eight or ten days, every year. He followed the Spiritual Exercises of Saint Ignatius Loyola, as every Jesuit has done once a year since the foundation of the Society in the sixteenth century. The first part of the Spiritual Exercises consists in prayer of repentance and acceptance of God's forgiveness, and Teilhard regularly spent the first two or three days of his annual retreat in prayer of sorrow for sin and receiving the Lord's forgiveness.

The following note comes from Teilhard's unpublished retreat notebooks now in the Jesuit house in Chantilly, outside Paris.

A reading from Teilhard

> (Meditation on the *Miserere* Psalm 51.) My sins seem to have little effect on me! Because I always rationalise so as to justify what I do... Nevertheless, in a confused and general way, I have every reason to humble myself before the adorable clear purity of Jesus Christ (1944 retreat, third day).

Prayerful considerations

Teilhard sees sin as looking for unity in the wrong way or in the wrong places. He writes to a friend: "What I think brings moral ruin to the people you describe is not that they take hold of matter, but that they take hold of it incompletely, by easy little bits, instead of approaching it resolutely in its total wealth, its sacred mystery, and its incomparable majesty. The pleasure-seeker makes a misuse of the tangible because he breaks it up into such tiny pieces that he sees himself as its master and possessor. Whereas, if he knew how to take an all-embracing look at the grandeur of what he is profaning, he would – on the contrary – fall on his knees. The fundamental evil that besets us... is our incapacity to see the whole. Add this new way of seeing things to the most disquieting tendencies of our time, and they would be changed into magnificent virtues. I some times get vague and undefined longings to gather a small group of friends around me and – through all the admitted conventions – give the example of a life in which nothing would count but the preoccupation with, and love for *all* the earth."[4]

Love gives unity. But love means going out of myself to another, unselfishly, and not possessing or using the other for my own gratification. However, sometimes I look instead for love in the wrong places or in the wrong way; I act possessively, selfishly, opposite from loving. Through sinning, I go against love. I move not in the direction of true unity but in the direction of break-down, of disunity, of multiplicity. Sin and love are, in Teilhard's view, exact opposites. And every sin is turning my back on the Lord, refusing union with him, refusing his love.

A sinner, I live in a world where evil, including sin, is simply a condition, a dimension of reality, inevitable. And, inevitably, although freely, I do sin. But I can repent, be sorry, turn to the Lord and accept his forgiveness.

- Like all Jesuits, Teilhard made an examination of conscience twice a day, repenting of his sins and faults and asking the Lord's forgiveness. Consider making a resolution to make an examination of conscience daily in the evening before going to bed. You could use four points: [1] Thank the Lord for the day so far. [2] Let him reveal to you your sins and faults, your failures to love. [3] Tell him you're sorry. [4] Accept his forgiveness and thank him for his mercy toward you.

- Take some prayer time for this: Divide your life into sections; for instance, infancy up to adolescence, adolescence, adulthood, recently. Then look at each period of time, making two prayerful considerations: [1] What has the Lord done for me in all of these periods of my life? Thank him for his goodness to you. [2] Remaining with the same period of time, look at your sins and sinfulness in that part of your life. Be sorry before the Lord, and accept his forgiveness.

- Read the Psalm below, under the title "God's Word", slowly and thoughtfully, pausing after each phrase, letting the prayer sink in, meaning it. Then put the text aside and humble yourself before the Lord, repentant and accepting his mercy and forgiveness. You might then repeat a short prayer over and over, like "My Jesus, mercy." Or, "Thank you, Jesus, for your forgiveness."

- During the day repeat often the short prayer, "Thank you, Jesus, for forgiving me."

God's Word

In your goodness, O God, have mercy on me;
with gentleness wipe away my faults.
Cleanse me of guilt;
free me from my sins.
My faults are always before me;
my sins haunt my mind.
I have sinned against you and no other –
knowing that my actions were wrong in your eyes.
Your judgement is what I deserve;
your sentence supremely fair.

As you know I was born in guilt,
from conception a sinner at heart.
But you love true sincerity,
so you teach me the depths of wisdom.
Until I am clean, bathe me with hyssop;
wash me until I am whiter than snow.
Infuse me with joy and gladness;
let these bones you have crushed dance for joy.
Please do not stare at my sins;
blot out all my guilt.
Create a pure heart in me, O my God;
renew me with a steadfast spirit.
Don't drive me away from your presence,
or take your Holy Spirit from me.
Once more be my Saviour; revive my joy.
Strengthen and sharpen my still weak spirit.
And I will teach transgressors your ways;
then sinners will return to you, too.
Release me from death, God my Saviour,
and I will announce your justice.
Open my lips,
and my tongue will proclaim your glory.
Sacrifices give you no pleasure;
if I offered a holocaust, you would refuse it.
My sacrifice is this broken spirit.
You will not disdain a contrite and humbled heart.
(Ps 51 – *Miserere*)

Closing prayer: Lord Jesus, I am sorry for my sins. I am sorry because I have sometimes justified myself and not taken responsibility for my sins. Give me the grace to be sorry and to accept your loving and merciful forgiveness.

4

Creation and co-creation

The grace I ask: To contribute to the process of creation by whatever I do that is positive; to co-operate with the creative action of Jesus Christ in the world.

Prayer: Lord Jesus, thank you for your continuous creation of the world and for your ongoing creation of me. I ask the grace to know better your personal love of me, that you call me by name, know me perfectly. Give me the grace to know the value of what I do in union with you.

Teilhard

By 1918, Teilhard had sent several of his essays, written at the front in times of peace and quiet, to his Jesuit provincial superior. Teilhard had been promoted from stretcher bearer to chaplain of the regiment, a post without rank in the French army. It gave him more time for prayer and reflection. And what he conceived, he wrote down, first in his small notebooks, and then in handwritten essays.

The Provincial and his staff had real problems with the essays, and especially with two entitled, *The Struggle against the Multitude,* and *Creative Union.* For one thing, the essays did not follow the theology of Saint Thomas Aquinas, at that time the only respectable guide for Catholic theology. For another, they seemed pantheistic, talking about the presence of Jesus Christ in the world through love. Was the world then identified with Jesus Christ? Did Teilhard confuse the Creator and his creatures? The provincial staff seemed unaware that Thomas Aquinas too, in his time, had been accused of pantheism.

Furthermore, Teilhard had a whole new idea of creation. Did he deny creation out of nothing? Did his new idea equal heresy? This marked the beginning of Teilhard's difficulties with his superiors, his failure to get permission to publish anything of a theological or spiritual nature, his eventual exile in China and in the United States, far from his beloved Paris where he could have had a greater intellectual influence.

In all this, Teilhard showed obedience: obedience to his superiors, obedience to the Church. His obedience depended on his understanding of creation and divine providence.

He understands creation not as an act that began the world, but as a process that goes on now, in the world, in our lives. The world is moving, going into a future that has as its end point the Second Coming of Jesus Christ. The world's movement forward, seen by us as evolution, social progress, technological advancement, the course of our own personal lives, is determined by God's creative action. He keeps things moving ahead, into the future. How? Through the creative love of Jesus drawing all things forward toward an eventual and final unity in him, when this world will end, the world will be reconciled in Christ, and he will hand it over to the Father, and God will be all in all.

The expression "Christ-Omega" is common in Teilhard's writings. He takes the word "Omega", the last letter of the Greek alphabet, from Christ's description of himself in the New Testament Book of Revelation as the Alpha and the Omega. Teilhard uses it to indicate that the risen Christ is the end, the end-point, of the world. He understands the world not as having been started off by a Creator in the past, but rather as being created by being drawn into the future by the Creator God acting in and through the risen humanity of Jesus. And Jesus stands ahead of us, in the future, Omega. He *is* the Future, the future of everyone and of the world, a future with a face. "When Christ appears in the clouds", Teilhard writes, "he will simply be manifesting a metamorphosis that has been slowly accomplished under his influence in the heart of the mass of mankind."[5]

A reading from Teilhard

> You have so filled the universe in every direction, Jesus, that from now on it is blessedly impossible for us to escape you. "Where can I go to escape your spirit, where to flee from your face?" Now I am quite certain. Neither life, whose progress reinforces the hold you have on me; nor death which throws me into your hands, nor the good or bad spiritual powers which are your living instruments; nor the energies of matter, into which you are plunged;... nor the unfathomable abysses of space, which are the measure of your greatness; neither death, nor life, nor angels, nor principalities, nor powers, nor forces, nor the

present, nor the future, nor height, nor depth, nor any creature (Rom 8:38) – none of these things will be able to separate me from your substantial love, because they are all only the veil, the "species", under which you hold me so that I can hold you. *(Le milieu divin,* Seuil, 1957, page 156.)

Prayerful considerations

The whole movement of the world, and all the parts and lines of development of that movement, are animated by Jesus risen, given life by him. The forward impetus of each thing in the universe comes from Jesus Christ who draws all things to himself without, however, disturbing the world's normal processes. Because Jesus has our humanity, and has become the central element in the universe, nothing is profane for those who know how to see.

Everything that we do, no matter how secular, how routine, has religious value. It contributes in some small way to building the world in the direction of Jesus who draws all things to himself. The labour I do participates in the creative process, is my small act of co-creation, co-operating with Jesus holding all things together in himself and through love drawing all things to himself. Even maintenance is a way of building; even sweeping the floor has religious value.

- What do you do? Do you work, keep house, study, teach? Whatever it is, consider in the light of this fact: this, your way of contributing to the reconciliation and unity of all things in Jesus Christ, however small, has importance, has real value beyond its obvious value. You co-create in your own small way, acting with Jesus. And he loves you in what you do, takes interest in it; it is important to him. Partly because you do it, and partly because what you do has its *own* importance.

- Make an offering to Jesus of yourself and of all you do. For example, here is a prayer of offering:

  "Lord Jesus, thank you for giving me this day. I offer to you my every thought, word, action, and suffering of this day. Amen."

  Or:

  "Jesus, I give you my every thought, word, action, joy and suffering of this day. Thank you for this day. Thank you for loving me."

- Make up your own prayer, or use one of the above prayers, or one that you already know. *Say it every morning when you get up.* The morning offering will orient your day and consecrate it to Jesus.

- Read the Scripture text below, from Paul's Letter to the Romans, considering each phrase and pausing after reading it. Leave the text from time to time to rest in the presence of Jesus quietly, relating to him in terms of the text, in silence, or repeating a short prayer over and over, like "Nothing can separate me from your love."

- During the day repeat a short prayer, "I offer to you, Lord, what I am doing now," or, "Jesus, I offer this to you."

God's Word

Can anything cut us off from the love of Christ? – can hardships or distress, or persecution, or lack of food and clothing, or threats of violence? As Scripture says, "For your sake we are being massacred all day long, treated as sheep to be slaughtered."

No, we come through all these things triumphantly victorious, by the power of him who loved us. For I am certain of this: neither death nor life, nor angels, nor principalities, nothing already in existence and nothing still to come, nor any power, nor the heights nor the depths, nor any created thing whatever, will be able to come between us and the love of God, known to us in Christ Jesus our Lord (Rom 8:35-39).

Closing prayer: "O Jesus Christ, you truly contain within your goodness and your humanity all the unyielding grandeur of the world. I love you as the source, the active and life-giving Surrounding, and... the centre at which all things meet and which stretches out over all things so as to gather them to itself. I love you for the extensions of your body and soul in all creation through grace, through life, and through matter. I love you *as a world,* as this world... Lord Jesus, you are the centre towards which all things move." *(Ecrits du temps de la guerre,* Seuil, 1976, page 59-60.)

5

The Eucharist

The grace I ask: To see Jesus present in the Eucharist as a centre of Love.

Opening prayer: Jesus, I thank you for the sacrament of the Eucharist, and I worship and adore you now in your presence in all the Masses going on at this moment in the world, and in your presence in all the tabernacles all over the world. Give me the grace to appreciate more your Eucharistic presence for me.

Teilhard

During the war, while at the front, Teilhard usually could not celebrate Mass. In those days, the Church did not allow a priest to say Mass outside a church or chapel, and so Teilhard often went several days without saying Mass or receiving Holy Communion. For his own private use, he wrote some quite long prayers that imitated in some ways the Mass. They substituted for the Mass as a kind of "dry Mass." These prayers became an essay, "The Priest".[6]

After the First World War, Teilhard studied at the University of Paris where he earned a doctorate in palaeontology, a science that deals with life in past geological periods as known from fossils. He remained in Paris teaching in the Catholic Institute there, doing research, and frequently meeting with young Catholic intellectuals to share his ideas and his spirituality. Because his Jesuit superiors considered several of his essays, even though unpublished, dangerous to Catholic orthodoxy and perhaps heretical, and because of the great influence that Teilhard and his ideas had on many graduate students, his superiors took action. They ordered him out of France, where his influence was so great.

They sent Teilhard to China in 1926, where he worked in his field of palaeontology, becoming one of the historical founders of Chinese geology and palaeontology. On frequent scientific expeditions into the interior of China in order to uncover fossil remains and study them, Teilhard found himself a long way from any Catholic church or chapel. Unable to say Mass, he used his essay, "The Priest," and in 1923 he rewrote it as, "The Mass on the World".[7] On expedition, just as he would daily go off alone to meditate and to pray the Divine Office in his breviary, so too Teilhard would disappear for a short time in order to celebrate his own "Mass" without altar, without bread or wine. Here is a part of his "offering prayer", between the readings and the main part of the Mass:

> Lord, I have neither bread nor wine nor altar, but I lift myself beyond these symbols up to the pure majesty of the Real, and I offer you... on the altar of the entire earth: the work and the suffering of the whole world. Receive, Lord, this entire host that your creation, moved by you yourself, offers you.[8]

Teilhard, of course, said Mass every day of his life that he could. The Eucharist had a central place in his life. He did not see it as cut off from everyday life and separate from the world. On the contrary, he recognised the Eucharist as central to reality.

A reading from Teilhard

The following applies to the consecration, the centre of the Mass: When Christ, extending the movement of his Incarnation, descends into the bread in order to replace it, his action does not limit itself to the small piece of matter that his presence will for a moment volatise and then transform. This transubstantiation surrounds itself with a real although attenuated divinization of the whole universe. From that cosmic element into which he inserts himself, the Word acts to subjugate and to assimilate all the rest. *(Ecrits du temps de la guerre,* op.sit. pages 287-288.)

When, through the mouth of the priest, Christ says, "This is my Body," these words overflow beyond the piece of bread over which they are said. They cause to be born the whole mystical Body. This priestly act extends even beyond the transubstantiated host to the Cosmos itself. (Quoted in the Introduction, *Hymne de l'univers,* op.sit. page 14.)

Prayerful considerations

- Spend some time before Jesus present in the Eucharist. Be aware that he is not only the centre, the heart of love, but that his love radiates out and enfolds you.

- Reflect on the Mass where Jesus' saving death is made present. His body is sacrificed to take away the sins of the world; his blood is poured out in a cleansing tide. Next time you are at Mass, offer the host for and with the whole of creation.
- At the Offertory of the Mass, offer yourself and your day, to be one with the continuing creative work of the Lord Jesus in the world.
- During the day repeat a short prayer, "Jesus, you see me and you love me; and you see and you love everyone and everything around me."

God's Word

Now as they were eating, Jesus took bread, and when he had said the blessing he broke it and gave it to the disciples. "Take it and eat," he said, "this is my body." Then he took a cup, and when he had given thanks he handed it to them saying, "Drink from this, all of you, for this is my blood, the blood of the covenant, poured out for many for the forgiveness of sins" (Mt 26:26-29).

Closing prayer: This prayer refers to Holy Communion: Grant, O Lord, that when I come to the altar for communion I may from now on be aware of the infinite perspectives hidden beneath the smallness and the nearness of the host in which you are concealed. I know that underneath the appearance of bread is a devouring power of love that, far from being consumed by me, consumes me… The Eucharist must invade my life. My life must become, as a result of the sacrament, an unlimited and endless contact with you. (Adapted from *The Divine Milieu,* Seuil, 1957 page 126.)

6

The cross of Jesus

The grace I ask: To comprehend that the suffering and death of Jesus constituted an act of love and redemption for me and for the world.

Prayer: Lord Jesus, help me to better understand the price you have paid for me, for my salvation, and for the salvation of the world, and to realise that you have done this out of love for me, personally, and for the world.

Teilhard

Teilhard's experience of suffering and death in the First World War came to a head near the end of the war. Teilhard's regiment of Zouaves, after a bad defeat and severe losses, went to counter-attack the Germans. The action took place in a cornfield near a forest in eastern France. And it was the worst action Teilhard had seen. Shells came down like hailstones. Low flying German aircraft strafed the cornfield. Soldiers of the regiment lay everywhere. Teilhard worked ceaselessly with the stretcher bearers to get the wounded to safety.

For the first time since the beginning of the war,

Teilhard seriously considered the possibility that he could be killed in battle. The four day engagement with the Germans badly shook him psychologically. He remained shaken until well after the war's tide turned when fresh troops came from America, the Germans went down in defeat, and the armistice was signed.

The experience of war, and especially of the battle in the cornfield, helped Teilhard to better understand the suffering and cross of Jesus, to know better its meaning. The French soldiers who suffered and who died in World War I fought, and therefore suffered and died, for France. They acted out of patriotism, however minimal, and however unfelt at the time. Patriotism is a form of love; it is love of one's country. The suffering and death of World War I was, then, not negative, but positive. The men and women who suffered and died did so out of love, at least out of love in some form. The horror of the war did not obscure this fact, but only made it clearer.

The ugly war experience made clearer to Teilhard the meaning of the cross. Jesus died out of love. "No one can have greater love than to lay down his life for his friends" (Jn 15:13). Jesus' life was not taken from him; he gave, he laid it down for each of us in particular, for all of us, for the world's salvation.

Furthermore, Jesus won. He lost the battle; they tortured him to death on the cross. But he won the war, the war for you, for each of us, for our salvation, for the world's salvation. He died that the world be saved, not, then, something negative. Rather, a hard and terribly difficult labour of love that cost Jesus pain and death.

In his suffering and death, Jesus bore not only the weight of our sins but the weight of the world's progress toward the end-time when he will come again, and when this world will come to an end and be transformed into the world to come. By his cross Jesus has the victory over sin, over all that oppresses us, over death itself. The cross, much more than simply a symbol of reparation and expiation, stands for progress and victory through suffering-love and difficult labour. The cross is the symbol of the synthesis of the "upward" component of sacrifice and adoring reparation, and the "forward" component of progress through laborious effort. In John's Gospel, Jesus speaks of his coming cross as his glorification. Teilhard came to see the cross of Jesus as a cross of glory.

A reading from Teilhard

Jesus is truly he who bears the sins of the world; moral evil is mysteriously compensated for by suffering. But more fundamentally, Jesus is he who structurally overcomes in himself, and for all of us, the resistance to spiritual ascent, a resistance inherent in matter.

God will make it good by making evil itself serve a higher good for those who are faithful to him. Like an artist who makes use of a fault or an impurity in the stone he sculpts or in the bronze he casts so as to produce more beautiful lines or a better shape and tone, so God, without sparing us the partial deaths nor the final death which form an essential part of our lives, transfigures them by integrating them into a higher and better plan, provided we lovingly trust in him. Not everything is immediately good to those who seek God, but everything can become good. (Adapted from several of Teilhard's essays, quoted in R. Faricy, *Teilhard de Chardin's Theology of the Christian in the World,* Sheed and Ward, 1967, pages 165-166 and 203.)

Prayerful Considerations

- Jesus calls me "friend" (Jn 15:15). "I shall no longer call you servants,... I call you friends." And for that reason he died for me with great love. "No one can have greater love than to lay down his life for his friends" (Jn 15:13).

- Jesus won life for me by going through death. My daily "deaths", diminishments of whatever kind, are the opening in me to Jesus' victory. "My grace is enough for you: for power (Jesus' power) is at full stretch in weakness" (2 Cor 12:9).

- Jesus says to me: "If anyone wants to be a follower of mine, let him renounce himself and take up his cross every day and follow me" (Lk 9:23). So my daily crosses, whatever they may be, labour, sufferings of any kind, when I take them up and follow Jesus on his Calvary road, make me a "partner of his triumph" (2 Cor 2:14), carrying my cross with him in his "triumphal procession" (Col 2:15).

- Reflect that the cross, once a symbol of disgrace, has since Jesus died on it, become a luminous beacon of hope, drawing us forward and upward, for Jesus said, "When I am lifted up from the earth, I shall draw all things to myself" (Jn 12:32).

- During the day repeat often the short prayer, "Lord, by your cross and resurrection, you have redeemed the world."

God's Word

"No one can have greater love than to lay down his life for his friends" (Jn 15:13).

"Father, the hour has come; glorify your Son… (Jn 17:1).

Then they crucified him and shared out his clothing, casting lots to decide what each should get. It was the third hour when they crucified him. The inscription giving the charge against him read, 'The King of the Jews.' And they crucified two bandits with him, one on his right and one on his left" (Mk 15: 24-27).

Closing prayer: Lord Jesus, you died for me personally, to save me, out of love for me, as though I were the only other besides you who ever walked on earth. And you would do it again if you had to. You laid down your life for me out of love.

7

The cross in my life

The grace I ask: To value the cross in my own life as a share in the cross of Jesus.

Prayer: Lord Jesus, I ask to understand the place of the cross in my life, and the grace to take up my cross and follow you.

Teilhard

Teilhard experienced much suffering in his life: psychological and emotional suffering: all his life he had anxiety, a free floating anxiety that sometimes became anguish. Physical suffering: in later life, a grave heart condition not only troubled Teilhard and eventually caused his death, but it made much more acute his anxiety, which now sometimes resulted in attacks that sent him to bed for a few days. Misunderstanding and rejection: his ideas, thought heretical by his Jesuit superiors and by several influential people in Rome, especially Jesuits, got him into trouble from the time of his early essays to his death. He put up with the psychological and the physical suffering; he knew its value, and he united it to the redemptive work of Jesus for the salvation of the world.

Especially in writings during the last two decades of his life, he speaks of his anxiety. In 1950, in a letter to a friend, Teilhard writes, "A surge of that nervous anxiety that is more or less my lot since birth (and that is picking up with age) has more or less slowed me down." And in a letter to his provincial superior in Paris in 1953, two years before his death of a heart attack in 1955, he writes, "For the past month I have been going through a phase of anxiety – the kind that, several times since 1940, comes periodically and makes my every effort extremely painful".[9] In his personal retreat notes, he speaks of his "physical anxiety" and his "vertigo of fragility, of instability". (Retreats of 1942 and 1945, unpublished.)

The rejection of his ideas, and so to a large extent of himself, by Church superiors caused him continuous and great suffering, and of course accentuated his anxiety. "Dear friend" he pleaded, in a letter to Auguste Valensin, a Jesuit confrère whom Teilhard counted "one of my best friends", "Please help me. I've put a good face on it outwardly, but within it is something that resembles an agony or a storm."[10] Most of his life, exiled not only from Europe and especially from Paris ("My roots are in Paris; cut off from those roots I lose the best of my energy,"[11]) and forbidden to publish any material of a religious, spiritual, or theological nature, he felt stymied and frustrated. A few Protestant friends urged him to leave the Catholic Church; some lay Catholic friends advised him to leave the priesthood; and one or two non-Jesuit priest friends suggested he leave the Jesuit order. In any of these cases he would have been able to publish his essays and books, and perhaps even able to return to

Paris. He loved the priesthood and certainly had a vocation from the Lord to be a priest. And there was no question of his leaving the Catholic Church or the Jesuits. "I see now more clearly and more concretely that nothing spiritual, nothing divine, can reach a Christian – or a religious – save through the intermediary of the Church – or of his order." That was in August 1925. Four years later it was the same: "The faintest idea of a move to leave the order has never crossed my mind" he could say in 1929.[12] Over two decades later he wrote to a long time friend, Lucille Swan, in 1949, "I feel just as deeply as before that the very motion of mankind which I perceive is toward the Christ who is in the Church; so that I cannot fight the Church or leave it!"[13]

But why did he remain all his life in the Jesuits, a faithful and completely obedient Jesuit? He could have legitimately obtained permission to leave; and he could have been relatively free to do what he felt called to do: make his ideas available to others.

He stayed because, like his anxiety, and like the physical suffering in his later life, life in the Jesuit order was a cross from the Lord. He wanted to carry it. He did not hold that staying in a religious order on principle, "to stay for the sake of staying," was a virtue. People could and did leave for good reasons.

But Teilhard knew he belonged in the Jesuits. God's plan for the world is an integral plan. Each of us is like a knot in a net, part of a larger fabric. For Teilhard to leave the Jesuits would have been to try to move a knot in a net. To be Jesuit was part of God's plan for Teilhard, and where he fit into God's larger plan. He writes, "I'm conscious of being very strongly bound to the Church and to the Jesuits for higher and always new reasons; I feel I would betray the world if I left the place assigned me. In this sense, I do love them, both the Church and the Jesuit order, and I want to work in my small way in them, within them. So be very certain that I have never seriously even entertained the idea of leaving the order."[14] Obedience in the order certainly was a cross for Teilhard; he carried it.

A reading from Teilhard

> The cross is no longer only the symbol of expiation, but also the sign of the growth that is accomplished in pain. Detachment no longer means exactly to despise and to reject, but instead to work through and to sublimate. Resignation and acceptance is the final form of the fight against evil, the transformation in God of inevitable defeats. (Quoted in R. Faricy, *Dimensions of the Future,* page 59.)
>
> The road our Saviour followed is the road of the cross, the road that each of us is called on to follow with him; the truth about our position in this world is that we are on the cross. And in Jesus crucified, each of us can recognise his own image. (Adapted from early writings, quoted in R. Faricy, 'Teilhard de Chardin's Spirituality of the Cross', in *Horizons,* vol. 3, 1976, page 9.)

Prayerful considerations

Whatever my cross is, whatever my crosses are, the Lord tells me that to be his disciple, I have to take up my cross and follow him. He does not suggest that I drag it behind me, nor that I kick it, nor that I hit other people over the head with it. Whether the cross is one of physical suffering, of age, of grief, of failure, of interior distress, or of rejection, carrying my cross is a positive act, an act of love, an act of loving sacrifice. It can be the hard work of changing what I can, or the discipline necessary for some kind of personal growth, or it can be the cross of accepting what I cannot change. In any case, I carry it with Jesus, united with him in his love for me.

- What is the cross in your life? What shape does the cross take for you? If more than one, what are they, in what do they consist? Take them one at a time, in prayer, and – with Jesus – unite them with his cross.

- Do you suffer interiorly now or habitually? If fear or fears attack you or stay with you, for example fear of death or of the future, or sadness or discouragement or depression, in prayer unite your interior suffering with that of Jesus in his agony in the garden before his crucifixion (Mt 26:36-46).

- Do you suffer physically or from rejection, from being made fun of, from darkness in prayer and from feeling that God is not there, that he has abandoned you? Turn to the Lord in prayer, and unite your suffering with his.

- Often during the day, offer whatever you do that might be difficult, that costs you something personally, and whatever suffering of any kind you undergo, to Jesus, uniting your work and your suffering and your renunciation with his cross. You could say a short prayer, like "Jesus, this is for you." Or make one up and repeat it during the day.

God's Word

Jesus said to his disciples, "If anyone wants to be a follower of mine, let him renounce himself and take up his cross and follow me. Anyone who wants to save his life will lose it; but anyone who loses his life for my sake will find it" (Mt 16:24-25).

Closing prayer: Lord Jesus, I unite the cross in my life with your cross, I unite all my sufferings, even the small ones, with your sufferings.

8

The cross, death, and growth

The grace I ask: The relief of knowing that the cross in my life has meaning, that it can unite me more closely with Jesus, and above all, that it helps me to grow in union with him.

Prayer: Lord Jesus, I ask to understand the meaning of the cross in my life, and the grace to take up my cross more generously and with more love, and to follow you better.

Teilhard

In later life, Teilhard suffered from a terrible fear of dying. His fear of death came partly from his anxiety condition and partly from the darkness in his prayer that made him feel as though death were the end and nothing existed after that.

In Teilhard's earlier essays and personal notes he considers death with a kind of scientific objectivity. Death is "the regular indispensable condition of the replacement of one individual by another".[15] At the same time it is our worst enemy, "the epitome and the common basis of everything that terrifies us".[16] Death is the "form *par excellence* of the inevitable, menacing, newness bringing future".[17] But Jesus, by his own death on the cross, has transformed death. In itself a total failure and an awful stumbling block, death now, conquered by the cross of Jesus, has the value of a metamorphosis, a transformation, a passage to a new life.

In his personal notes, however, especially in the later part of his life, Teilhard underlines the negative aspect of the cross, by which it stands for a share in the death of Jesus. He writes, for his own eyes only, in his (unpublished) notes from his retreats from 1941 to 1954 about his fear of death. Death "opens out into the unknown". "To what degree does death kill our taste for living? In fact, we live in forgetfulness of death, and when death approaches, we lose the taste for living, or at least we risk losing it." Teilhard has two anxiety provoking questions: after death, "Will Jesus be there?" and "Will he accept me or reject me?" He writes, "The second question should encourage and challenge me, but it makes me afraid instead." "Nothing would be hard if I were sure that there is a Jesus on the other side." And he writes of the rise of the old fear, "that there is Nothing on the other side."[18]

The fear of death as dead-end is never absent in the notes from Teilhard's last ten retreats. But the fear on the surface is always balanced by something deeper and expressed more often and more strongly in his notes: an unshakeable faith and trust in the Lord. "Alone in retreat, and alone at death; God has to be faced centre to centre, person to person." "The difficult thing, in old age, is to get used to the idea of life *without a future* for me. Face to the wall. And yet, as so many interests tend to evaporate (as death approaches), a higher interest binds them together."

In his retreat ten years before his death, he writes about advancing age as "diminution undergone in communion," and he adds a resolution "to accept, to love, interior fragility and ageing, with the shadows, and with the spaces ahead always shorter." In the end, he knows death is a communion with the Lord, and the meaning of the cross is that it marks a passage through death to Jesus. "Oh that I might drown in you, universal Jesus by trust now in this present instant... Oh Jesus, that I be not just a clanging cymbal. Oh Jesus, help me to end well."[19]

A reading from Teilhard

> When my body (and even more my spirit) begins to wear out and to show signs of age; when the evil that diminishes me or stands to carry me off strikes from without or comes to birth within me; when the painful moment comes in which I suddenly become aware that I am sick or growing old; and especially at that last moment when I feel that I am losing my grip and find myself absolutely passive in the hands of those great unknown forces that have formed me; in all those dark hours, O God, let me understand (granted that my faith be sufficient) that it is you who are painfully separating the fibres of my being in order to penetrate to the very marrow of my substance so as to carry me away into yourself...
>
> Teach me so that my *death may become an act of communion*. (*Le milieu divin*, op.sit. pages 95-96.)

Prayerful considerations

- Death as a passage from this life to Jesus in the next life follows the pattern of Jesus' own life, death, and resurrection. The Lord grew in age, grace, and wisdom. He died on the cross. He rose again. His death was a passage to the transformation of his resurrection, to his present glorified state.

By his death, he conquered death itself and transformed it. My death will be a share in his, and so a passage to a new life in and with him in the world to come.

- The pattern, then, is this: building up, death, resurrection. My first duty is find and build and become myself, to grow as a person, to develop myself. This, of course, is a lifetime programme, to develop personally, to unify my ideas and feelings and behaviour, to grow as a person.

    The second step is, in some form, some kind of death. I cannot reach the limits of personal development or arrive at a personal maturity without going out of myself and uniting with others. Jesus tells me that if I possess something, leave it and follow him. I have to lose myself for the sake of the kingdom in order to find myself. Only through the cross of some kind of death, of renunciation, of discipline, and of sacrifice in love, can I grow. Furthermore, crosses enter my life in the form of rejection, pain, failure, sickness, grief, discouragement; many of these seem to have no meaning, make no sense. They are the deaths that bring me down, break up the provisory unity of self, seemingly set me back. They, too, are in some way deaths, analogous to my coming death. They help me to die to myself.

    The third step: Re-centring. When I accept and carry my cross in union with the Lord, he puts together the fragmented pieces of my broken self to form a new unity, this time more centred on him and less on myself. My whole life, then, is a participation in the dying and rising of Jesus. My life stands in the structure of the life, death, and resurrection of the Lord.

- The sufferings and setbacks of everyday life are small crosses to be offered and carried; be ready for them when they come; accept, offer, and carry them in union with the Lord when they happen to you. They can unite you more closely with him.

- Make up a prayer to repeat often during the day. Or use this one: "Jesus, into your hands I commend my spirit."

God's Word

I have been crucified with Christ and yet I am alive; yet it is no longer I, but Christ living in me. The life that I am now living, subject to the limitation of human nature, I am living in faith, faith in the Son of God who loved me and gave himself for me" (Gal 2:20).

Closing prayer: Jesus, teach me to recognise the cross in my daily life, and to carry it in union with you.

9

Redemption and co-redemption

The grace I ask: To share in the redemptive work of Jesus by carrying the cross in my life in union with him.

Prayer: Lord Jesus, help me to understand that the cross in my life, carried in union with you, is productive, shares in your work of redemption and helps it, makes my sufferings and trials co-redemptive.

Teilhard

In his sixty-sixth year, in Paris for some months, Pierre Teilhard de Chardin had a serious heart attack. On the evening of the last day of May, Teilhard returned to his Jesuit community late and tired, told his brother priests that he wanted to go straight to his room to finish his prayers and go to bed, and climbed the stairs.

He awoke at dawn terrified. Wide awake, he felt a severe pain round his chest and running down his left arm. He could not get out of bed. He felt a lack of air, and difficulty in breathing. They took Teilhard to the hospital. His superior joined him at the hospital and asked, "Are you in pain?" Teilhard answered, "No." The superior asked, "Are you happy?" Teilhard again said "No."

The close brush with death changed Teilhard, and his heart condition, worse now, never really got better. From the hospital, he wrote to an old friend; in the letter he said, "It takes all of my philosophy and all of my faith to make constructive use of this terrible event."[20]

Teilhard had integrated his suffering into his relationship with Jesus Christ, appreciated its redemptive value, offered it to the Lord. And that appreciation and that offering took all of his philosophy and drew on all of his faith. The offering did not lessen the suffering. It did use the suffering, make it meaningful and a contribution to Jesus' redemptive work.

A reading from Teilhard

> The cross should be to us not just a sign of escape but of forward movement; the cross should shine before us not just as purifying but as motivating. The cross stands for the creative but laborious effort of humanity climbing toward Christ who awaits it. The cross is the symbol not only of the dark and regressive aspect of the universe, but also and above all of the luminous and conquering aspect; it is the symbol of progress and victory through difficult labour. The cross is the symbol, the way, the very act of progress. (Adapted from several of Teilhard's essays, quoted in R. Faricy, *Teilhard de Chardin's Theology of the Christian in the World,* op.sit. page 171.)
>
> Toward the peaks, shrouded in mist from our human eyes, whither the cross beckons us, we rise by a path which is the way of universal progress. The royal road

of the cross is no more nor less than the road of human endeavour supernaturally righted and prolonged. Once we have fully grasped the meaning of the cross, we are no longer in danger of finding life sad and ugly. We shall simply have become more attentive to its barely comprehensible solemnity. *(The Divine Milieu,* Collins, London, 1960, pages 103-104.)

Prayerful considerations

- Reflect that suffering is inevitable, but we can suffer with Jesus. "The sufferings of Christ overflow into our lives; so too does the encouragement we receive through Christ" (2 Cor 1:5). "Do not be taken aback at the testing by fire which is taking place among you, as though something strange were happening to you; but in so far as you share in the sufferings of Christ, be glad, so that you may enjoy a much greater gladness when his glory is revealed" (1 Pet 4:12-13).

- Look at Jesus, and see what he set out to do for me, from his "emptying himself" as equal to God (cf. Phil 2:6), his incarnation, his life of daily work, to his passion and death by crucifixion. "You have been bought at a price" (1 Cor 6:20).

- Yet he has left a part for me to do, in redemption. Saint Paul explains this when he writes "It makes me happy to be suffering for you now, and in my own body to make up all the hardships that still have to be undergone by Christ for the sake of his body, the Church" (Col 1:24). Christ still suffers, but now in me. Suffering and daily toil bring me closer to Jesus; they can be integrated into my growing relationship with him. "that I may come to know him and the power of his resurrection, and partake of his sufferings by being moulded to the pattern of his death, striving towards the goal of resurrection from the dead" (Phil 3:10).

- Reflect that suffering is an evil in itself, but can be turned to use. It can be reparation for our bringing evil into creation. "Christ suffered for you and left an example for you to follow his steps. He had done nothing wrong..." (1 Pet 2:21-22). It can end sin in my life. "As Christ has undergone bodily suffering, you too should arm yourselves with the same conviction that anyone who has undergone bodily suffering has broken with sin, because for the rest of life on earth that person is ruled not by human passions but only by the will of God" (1 Pet 4:1).

- As suffering is an evil in itself, we are free to struggle against it, as Jesus did in Gethsemane when he sweated blood in agony of mind, and prayed, "Father, take this cup from me" (Mk 14:36). And "He offered up prayer and entreaty, aloud and in silent tears, to the one who had the power to save him out of death" (Heb 5:7). Normally, suffering is to be escaped from if possible, until it becomes evident that this is what God wants. Then we look to Jesus who "learned obedience through sufferings" (Heb 5:8). Struggle, doubt, and detestation of suffering do not detract from its redemptive value when these are united with the agony of Jesus.

- My part is not just co-creation, but co-redemption, with Jesus. What I do and in a special way what I undergo, matters, helps, saves, redeems in and with Jesus Christ redeeming. I make up what is lacking in his suffering, the suffering that redeems the world. By the small daily deaths I undergo, I contribute to his great project of the world's salvation.

- During the day repeat often the short prayer, "All for you, Jesus." Or just offer up to the Lord, when they happen, whatever setbacks or failures, or irritations or rejections, you might have today.

God's Word

It makes me happy to be suffering for you now, and in my own body to make up all the hardships that still have to be undergone by Christ for the sake of his body, the Church, of which I was made a servant with the responsibility towards you that God gave to me, that of completing God's message, the message which was a mystery hidden for generations and centuries and has now been revealed to his holy people. It was God's purpose to reveal to them how rich is the glory of this mystery among the gentiles; it is Christ among you, your hope of glory: this is the Christ we are proclaiming, admonishing, and instructing every one in all wisdom, to make everyone perfect in Christ. And it is for this reason that I labour, striving with his energy which works in me mightily (Col 1:24-27).

Closing prayer: Lord Jesus, I offer to you my own pain, sufferings, loneliness, rejection, my grief or sadness. And also my struggles, my hard work, my labour. I know that, offered to you, they help make up what is wanting, lacking, in your sufferings for the redemption of the world. My suffering has value, the value of redemption, of co-redeeming with you. I offer it to you, Jesus.

10

The Lord is risen

The grace I ask: Risen Jesus, you are here present to me now, I want you to be the centre of my life.

Prayer: Lord Jesus, you are risen and in your place as the centre of the world and the centre of my life.

Teilhard

Teilhard liked Easter because he liked the mystery of the resurrection of Jesus. The Jesus of Teilhard's life, the Jesus he prayed to and turned to during the day, the Jesus who gave him the peace so many people felt in him and coming from him, was the risen Christ, the Jesus of the resurrection, risen once, here now risen, and coming again in his glory. Jesus, the Christ of the resurrection, was like the air Teilhard breathed; he lived in the presence of the risen Christ. He did not, however, always feel that presence; at some periods of his life he felt the absence of Jesus even in the faith knowledge of his presence. "His holy presence ought gradually to absorb me. Here's the point: I feel myself really in conflict, as if that presence, precisely, were less present to me. That these days, (of retreat, 1948) gently, put me back in him, to him!"[21]

In his annual retreats, making the Spiritual Exercises of Saint Ignatius Loyola for eight to ten days, Teilhard followed faithfully the quite structured retreat framework laid down by Ignatius. But, when the time came to pray about Jesus' resurrection, we know from his unpublished retreat notes that Teilhard always substituted reflection about and prayer to Jesus present through his creative love in the world. For Teilhard, the resurrection was not just a past event. It was Jesus risen present to him in and through the world now.

On 9 April 1955, the Saturday just before Easter, Teilhard went to confession to a Jesuit friend. Shortly before, he had told a cousin in the French diplomatic mission to the United States, Jean de Lagarde, that he would like "to die on the day of the Resurrection".[22] The next day, Easter Sunday, a beautiful spring day, Teilhard said his Mass as he always did. Then he went to Saint Patrick's Cathedral to attend the Pontifical High Mass because he wanted to celebrate the resurrection of Jesus in a special way. His health and his spirits were good. He continued to celebrate the resurrection by walking through Central Park and going to a concert in the afternoon. After the concert, he visited a friend, Rhoda de Terra, the wife of his deceased friend and co-worker Helmut de Terra, for tea in her apartment. Standing, he lifted the cup of tea to his lips and fell full length on the floor. He had a massive cerebral haemorrhage. By the time an American priest had come to give him the last rites, Teilhard had died.

Only a few people came to the funeral on Easter Tuesday. Teilhard was buried in white Mass vestments, white for the resurrection, in the Jesuit cemetery at Saint

Andrew's on the Hudson, sixty miles north of New York City, far from France and from his beloved Paris. But by the time of his burial he was already at home with the risen Jesus.

Not just the Holy Communion of the Mass was communion for Teilhard. Not even only his prayer. Life was communion with Jesus risen. And so was death.

When he died, Teilhard was known, especially in New York, only as a priest and a scientist, not as a mystic and a great spiritual and philosophical writer. His works had for the most part not been published yet. Since his death, his writings have taught hundreds of thousands of Christians to live and to die in communion with Christ risen.

Luisa Rahner, the mother of the great Catholic theologian Karl Rahner, died in 1976 at the age of 101. In her prayer book she had written a prayer copied from Teilhard's writings; it appeared on the memorial holy card passed out at her funeral. Here is the prayer: Lord, grant me something more precious still than the grace for which all the faithful pray. It is not enough that I should die just after having received Holy Communion. Teach me to treat my death as an act of Communion.[23]

A reading from Teilhard

> Jesus Christ has conquered death, not only by suppressing its evil but also by reversing its sting. Because of the Resurrection, nothing any longer kills necessarily. Everything is capable of becoming the blessed touch of the divine hands, the blessed influence of God's will. *(Le milieu divin,* op.sit. page 84.)

Prayerful considerations

- When Teilhard made his annual retreat, when he came to the part of the Spiritual Exercises in which he should have prayed about the resurrection of Jesus as an event, he prayed instead to Jesus present now in his resurrected state. And he applied the facts of Jesus' resurrection to his own relationship with Jesus now. You can do the same for your prayer.

    In praying about the resurrection, Ignatius of Loyola, the founder of the Jesuit order, suggests that you consider how Jesus acts in the post-resurrection appearances to Mary Magdalene and to the other disciples. Jesus acts as consoler; and he says, "Peace be with you," and "Fear not, it is I." You can pray about the resurrection the way that Teilhard did, not meditating on it as a fact that happened to Jesus, but going to the One it happened to, in his resurrected state, present to you now. Go to Jesus risen now, and let him affirm you, console you, support you, give you his peace, take away any fears or anxiety or sadness that you might have. Talk to him in your own words, or just be there with him, quietly, or perhaps repeating his name slowly.

- In receiving Jesus risen, in the Eucharist, I receive the fullness of his risen, divine life, according to my capacity. "In him, in bodily form, lives divinity in all its fullness" (Col 2:9). This is the risen Lord who lives in me. If he is the centre of my life, I can say with Saint Paul, "Life to me is Christ" (Phil 1:21).

- My Communions will one day come to a final and complete communion with Jesus in death and resurrection. "If we have been joined to him by dying a death like his, so we shall be by a resurrection like his" (Rom 6:5).

- Often during the day repeat the short prayer, "Thank you, Jesus, for being here." Or, from time to time, repeat a few times silently the name "Jesus", recognising him as present to you.

- Read the Scripture text in the next paragraph, "God's Word", slowly. Then put the text aside and be with Jesus present and loving you. Speak to him in your own words. Ask him questions. Or just be quiet in his presence. Keep the text at hand in case you have distractions; you can always go back to the text and it will turn you to Jesus.

God's Word

Jesus himself stood among them and said to them, "Peace be with you!" In a state of alarm and fright, they thought they were seeing a ghost. But he said, "Why are you so agitated, and why are these doubts stirring in your hearts? See by my hands and feet that it is I myself" (Lk 24:36-38).

Closing prayer: "Lord Jesus, may my being, in its self-offering to you, become ever more open and ever more transparent to your influence! And in that way may I feel your activity coming always closer, your presence always more intense, everywhere around me." (Adapted from: Teilhard, *Hymn of the Universe,* Collins, 1965, page 136.)

11

Jesus is Lord

The grace I ask: To love and follow Jesus who is Lord. To know the risen Jesus as Lord of all; and that this Lord of all things is, and wants to be to me always more, the loving Lord of my life.

Prayer: Jesus, you are Lord of heaven and of earth, of all things. I profess you as Lord, as my Lord and my God, and I take you again as the Lord of my life.

Teilhard

The slogan from the New Testament, and from New Testament times, that "Jesus is Lord," sums up in a short phrase Pierre Teilhard de Chardin's understanding of Jesus Christ, of who he is and of what he does. The Church still proclaims that "Jesus is Lord," as it has from the beginning. Teilhard de Chardin's understanding of the lordship of Jesus, as we find it in his writings, his private journals and retreat notes, and as we know he prayed it, was a radical and thoroughgoing appreciation of the relation of the universe and of each of us to the risen Jesus.

Pierre Teilhard de Chardin came to understand the lordship of Jesus over all things and over each thing and each person as far more than a juridical title. Jesus is Lord not just because he did a good job on earth and so the Father gave him a title above every other title, "Lord". Teilhard explains that the lordship of the risen Christ has a positively *organic* quality. Jesus is Lord because his incarnation, death, and resurrection have inserted him into the totality of reality as its lynch-pin; as the foundation stone of the universe, as he in whom all things hold together and without whom nothing would exist. Take Jesus away, and you would have nothing; all things exist in him and through him, through his love.

Jesus has dominion, sovereignty, rule, over each and all. And his dominion, his sovereignty, is a rule of love. His love holds the world and each part of it together in existence, and moves them forward.

In 1924, Pope Pius XI issued a papal encyclical on Christ the King. In his retreat notes for the retreat of 1940, Teilhard writes, "I've just re-read the encyclical on Christ the King. What a disillusionment! How static! Juridical! How inferior to the development in Paul's Letter to the Colossians!"[24]

In an essay written in Beijing, China, in 1942, Teilhard fully agrees with the teaching on Christ the King; the risen Christ is truly Lord of the universe. But he finds that Church teaching on Christ the King does not go far enough, does not sufficiently bring out the fullness of the lordship, of the kingship, of the dominion, of Jesus Christ. The following quotation from that essay expresses Teilhard's understanding of Jesus' Lordship.

A reading from Teilhard

Recently, Rome has made a gesture expressing a decisive stage in the development of dogma. It has translated and consecrated the irresistible current of Christian consciousness toward a more all-encompassing and realistic appreciation of the Incarnation. It has done this in the form of a statement about Christ the King.

My idea, my dream, is this: that the Church, by a logical prolongation of that same current, do what Saint Paul did for his converts: make explicit and show to the world the great figure of him in whom the fullness of being finds its real principle, its expression, and its substance: Christ Omega, the universal Christ. "He has descended and he has ascended to fill all things" (Eph 4:9-10). No doubt the meaning of this image remained unclear for the Romans, the Corinthians, the Ephesians, and the Colossians, because at that time "the world" and "the whole of reality" (with all the connotations of the organic that these words have for us today) did not yet have a place in human consciousness. But for us, fascinated by the newly discovered magnitude of the universe, Paul's image expresses exactly that divine aspect which suits our adoration. Christ the King, the universal Christ: between these two perhaps a subtle difference, but one that has great importance: the difference between an external power necessarily static and juridical, and an internal dominion that begins with matter and culminates in Grace, and that works on us by and through all the organic connections of the world-in-progress. *(Les directions de l'avenir,* Seui, 1973, pages 107-108.)

Prayerful considerations

- Jesus wants to be the Lord of your whole life, of everything in it, of the relationships and the problems and the situations in your life. He is interested in everything that interests you; nothing is too small or too silly. Your weight problem, your health, your work or studies, your hurt feelings, your resentments, your discouragement, your housing problem, your employment situation, Jesus cares about all those. Put them in his hands under his lordship; make him Lord of all of it. Go to Jesus in prayer, and look at what is on your mind, one thing at a time, and put it firmly and confidently with trust in his love, in his hands, under his lordship.

- Jesus is Lord of my life by right, not by my choosing. "God raised him high, and gave him the name [Lord] which is above all other names; so that all beings in the heavens, on earth and in the underworld should bend the knee at the name of Jesus and that every tongue should acknowledge Jesus Christ as Lord" (Phil 2:9-11).

- Christ is God and King of not just this world, but of all that is: "He is the image of the unseen God… for in him were created all things… everything visible and everything invisible… all things were created through him and for him. He exists before all things and in him all things hold together" (Col 1:15-17). I was created by him, and for him. He holds me together, "Sustaining all things by his powerful command" (Heb 1:3).

- Reflect on what follows from Jesus' lordship in my life, a lordship of love. Saint Paul writes, "As you received Jesus as Lord and Christ, now live your lives in him, be rooted in him, held firm by the faith you have been taught, and overflowing with thanksgiving" (Col 2:6).

- During the day frequently call upon the Lord, saying, "Lord Jesus."
- Read the Scripture text in the next paragraph, "God's Word". Be with the Lord Jesus; speak to him in your own words, or remain quiet with him. Go back to the text when you have a distraction, and let the Scripture passage return you to Jesus.

God's Word

Jesus Christ..., being in the form of God, did not count equality with God something to be grasped. But he emptied himself, taking the form of a slave, becoming as human beings are; and being in every way like a human being, he was humbler yet, even to accepting death, death on a cross. And for this God raised him high, and gave him the name which is above all other names; so that all beings in the heavens, on earth and in the underworld, should bend the knee at the name of Jesus and that every tongue should acknowledge Jesus Christ as Lord, to the glory of God the Father (Phil 2:6-11).

Closing prayer: Lord Jesus, you are the Lord of all things. You are the Lord of everything around me, and of everyone in my life. Your lordship is a lordship of love; thank you for loving me and for loving those that are dear to me. I profess you again as Lord, as my Lord and my God, and once again I take you as the Lord of my life. Amen.

12

Mary, the Mother of Jesus

The grace I ask: That I may know and appreciate Mary's place in my life: The Blessed Virgin Mary, the Mother of God, has an important role in my life. She is my mother in the spiritual order. And she stands for the whole feminine dimension of reality in my life, including the Church and that particular part of the Church that I belong to.

Prayer: Mary, you are my mother. You nurture me and give me life, and you lead me to a closer union with Jesus Christ.

Teilhard

Teilhard had great devotion to the Blessed Virgin Mary. He prayed the rosary every day, contemplating Jesus and Mary in the mysteries. In 1918, during the First World War, a village parish priest asked him to preach on the rosary one Sunday when his regiment had a rest behind the lines. Teilhard summarised his sermon in a letter to his cousin, Marguerite:

The rosary is an expansion, a further explanation, of

the Hail Mary... The Hail Mary is first of all an expression, primarily intuitive and from the heart, of love for Our Lady; and it helps us. It becomes a need to know Our Lady better and to be with her heart to heart... We relive the mysteries, so that the totality of Christian doctrine becomes familiar, concrete and real, in *Mary*. And we understand that the mysteries have their parallel... in our own joys and sorrows. So, in a way, our whole life is christianised in the development within us of the Hail Mary.[25]

In his annual retreat in October of 1943, Teilhard de Chardin, as he often did in his retreats, devoted one day to Our Lady, in this case the sixth day of an eight day retreat. This is really not in accord with the letter of the Spiritual Exercises of Saint Ignatius, but certainly not against the spirit of the Exercises. Teilhard often dedicated one day of an annual retreat to Mary because she had an important role in his life.

And yet, in those retreats where Teilhard gave a day to the Mother of Jesus, he rarely prayed to her or even about her. She was simply there, in his life, and he was conscious of her presence. He sometimes prayed that she would be more real in his life. He prayed to her sometimes, but apparently, judging from his retreat notes, not often. For example, in the 1943 retreat, for the day on Mary, in two pages of notes about the Kingdom of God and the Lordship of Jesus, he has only two lines saying that he prayed about the wedding feast at Cana, and that he has to stay in contact with Our Lord and with Our Lady because they give him life. (unpublished retreat notes, 1943, sixth day). In the 1948 retreat he has the cryptic note: "Mary's presence: Sacred Heart"; this seems to mean, in the context, that the Blessed Virgin, present in his life, leads him to the heart of Jesus. Similarly, the

1950 retreat has the notation, "Heart of Mary" with a line leading upward to the phrase, "Heart of Jesus."

The notes for the sixth day of Teilhard's 1944 retreat contain reflections on the "three feminines": the Church, the Jesuit order, and the Blessed Virgin Mary. He writes that he remains greatly attached, obviously, to the Church. "But," he adds in his notebook intended for his own eyes only, "what can I do when ninety per cent of her official representatives and ninety per cent of her pronouncements interfere with what I hold sacred, sacred because of that same Church, and the same for the Jesuit order?"

This is more than a reflection of Teilhard de Chardin's difficulties with authorities in the Church and in his order because of his ideas. He here manifests his suffering in the Church because the Church is not yet what she should be, not yet grown to be what in God's plan she should be structurally in the world and in our lives. But his attachment to her remains undiminished. He feels the same way about his own religious order, the Jesuits. His order and his Church are mothers, and not really good ones; but his attachment to them stays strong.

On the same notebook page, right after dealing with the Church and the Jesuit order, he writes about the "third feminine," the Blessed Virgin Mary. He calls her the face and the feminine influence of all progress.

For Teilhard, Mary represents the importance and even the priority of passivity, of passively receiving the love of Jesus Christ without acting. To pray passively, in contemplative prayer, and to accept unavoidable suffering offering it to the Lord: these for Teilhard are more important than acting. They are receiving from the Lord more than we could possibly ever give him.

Mary stands for that active passivity that is contemplative prayer and that is undergoing suffering especially in her Immaculate Conception, the doctrine that she was conceived in her mother's womb without any sin. In a letter, Teilhard writes about the December 8, feast day, the feast of the Immaculate Conception, saying that it is to him... the feast of "immobile activity," by which I mean activity that, through us, simply transmits the divine energy. In spite of appearances, purity is an essentially active virtue, because it concentrates God in us and brings God to those who are subject to our influence. In Our Lady, all modes of lower and disordered activity disappear in this single and luminous function of attracting and receiving God and allowing him to pass through her. To be active in that way and to that degree, the Blessed Virgin must have received her being in the very heart of grace – no subsequent justification, however precipitous, could replace this constitutive, inborn perfection of a purity that watched over even the coming to be of her soul. So, that is how I understand the Immaculate Conception.[26]

Have you ever thought about the meaning of the mystery of the Incarnation? When the time came for God to perform the Incarnation, he first had to make appear in the world a virtue capable of drawing himself down to us. He needed a Mother who would bear him in human surroundings. So what did he do? He created the Virgin Mary. That is to say, he caused to appear on earth a purity so great that, in its transparency, he would concentrate himself even to the point of coming as a little baby.[27]

As early as his war years Teilhard had seen the place of the Virgin Mary in his cosmic vision of Christ as the end point – Christ, as he said "in the fullness of his form".

"The world's energies and substances – so harmoniously adapted and controlled that the supreme

Transcendent would seem to germinate entirely from their immanence – concentrated and were purified in the stock of Jesse. From their accumulated and distilled treasures they have produced the glittering gem of matter, the Pearl of the Cosmos, and the link with the incarnate personal Absolute – the Blessed Virgin Mary, Queen and Mother of all things. When the day of the Virgin came to pass, then the final purpose of the universe, deep-rooted and gratuitous, was suddenly made clear."[28]

Pierre Teilhard de Chardin wrote only one essay about the Blessed Virgin Mary, in 1918, during the period of his early essays and the beginnings of his religious ideas. The title, "The Eternal Feminine," suggests the poetic and even allegorical nature of the writing.[29] The essay is in the first person; the "Eternal Feminine" speaks about herself in words that remind the reader of Wisdom, the personification of divine wisdom, in the books of the Old Testament. The Eternal Feminine stands for creation through unification. She says, finally, "I am the Church, the Bride of Christ." And "I am Mary, the Virgin, the Mother of all humankind" (pages 200-201). The "Eternal Feminine," the reader understands at the end of the essay, has all along been Mary, the Mother of Jesus.

The eternal feminine of the essay is not an allegorical figure, nor an abstraction. She is a "concrete universal." Not that the abstract principle of "the feminine" is concretised in Mary. Rather, that Mary in her personal individuality is universalised in the feminine, wherever it exists, and it exists universally.

A reading from Teilhard

> Mary is the face and the feminine influence of the progress that takes place in Christ, in my life and in the world. I want to recognise her more in my life. (Adapted from *Teilhard's unpublished retreat notes, 1944, sixth day.*)

Prayerful considerations

Mary is our mother, the mother of each one of us in the spiritual order. She leads us to Jesus. Do not be afraid that if you pray to her you will somehow be neglecting God. Mary always leads to Jesus.

- Say the rosary. The rosary is a contemplative prayer, non-conceptual, not really a vocal prayer. It is a prayer of contemplating the mysteries, of looking at them. There is the activity of repeating the prayers; this helps to avoid distractions. But the real prayer part is contemplative, passive.
- If you have not been praying the rosary, you might think about using it, *not* concentrating on the words of the prayers, but *looking* at whatever mystery you are on at the time. If you do not know how to pray the rosary, ask someone who does to teach you, or find a pamphlet or book that shows you how.
- Mary is the mother of Jesus who is "the eldest of many brothers" (Rom 8:29). So she is my mother in the order of grace; the mother of my spiritual life, with all that this relationship implies.
- Mary never promotes herself. Her only aim is to bring us to Jesus, and Jesus to us, to effect that

meeting and relationship. Pray to her for a growing knowledge of her Son, "Show to us the blessed fruit of your womb, Jesus."

- During the day sometimes turn to Mary for help, saying, "Mary, my mother, pray for me, help me."
- Read the Scripture text in the next paragraph, "God's Word." After reading it, put the text aside and be with Mary and Jesus present and loving you. Speak to them in your own words, first to Mary, and then – through her intercession and with her – to Jesus. Or, just be quiet in the presence of Mary, or of Jesus, or of both together.

God's Word

There was a wedding at Cana of Galilee. The mother of Jesus was there, and Jesus and his disciples had also been invited. And they ran out of wine, since the wine provided for the feast had all been used, and the mother of Jesus said to him, "They have no wine." Jesus said, "Woman, what do you want from me? My hour has not come yet." His mother said to the servants, "Do whatever he tells you." There were six stone water jars standing there, meant for the ablutions that are customary for the Jews: each could hold twenty or thirty gallons. Jesus said to the servants, "Fill the jars with water," and they filled them to the brim. Then he said to them, "Draw some out now and take it to the president of the feast." They did this; the president tasted the water and it had changed to wine. Having no idea where it came from – though the servants who had drawn the water knew – the president of the feast called the bride groom and said, "Everyone serves good wine first and the worse wine when the guests are well wined; but you have kept the best wine until now" (Jn 2:1-10).

Closing prayer: Mary, my mother, you are the mother that Jesus gave to me when he gave you to John at the time of his death on the cross. Pray for me now, and pray with me. Take me to Jesus.

Lord Jesus, I come to you with your mother, the mother you have given to me. Help me to recognise her presence in my life more, and to know her better. Help me through her to live more in union with you, and to know you better. Amen.

13

The universal Christ

The grace I ask: To see that through his love for all creation and for each element in creation, the risen Jesus makes himself present to all creation and to each element of it.

Prayer: Lord Jesus, you are everywhere, present to each part of the universe. You are present to me now through your personal love for me.

Teilhard

In his writings and also in his spiritual journals and retreat notebooks Teilhard speaks of "the Universal Christ." The universal Christ is the same Jesus of Nazareth, who died for us and who has risen, understood according to his presence everywhere in the universe through his love. "Christ clothed his person in the most sensible and most intimate charms of human individuality. He adorned that humanity with the most entrancing and most masterful splendours of the universe. And he came among us as the synthesis, surpassing all hope, of all perfection, such that every man was necessarily obliged to see and feel his presence, either to hate him, or to love him."

"As soon as he had appeared, a thrill passed through the seething mass of mankind that made it tremble in every fibre. It vibrated as one whole – since a multitude of the elect was already isolating itself in the midst of the multitude that still persisted, in spite of everything, in wandering aimlessly. In serried ranks, those who had freely chosen fidelity gathered around the Shepherd whose voice, like an assurance of life, echoed deep in their hearts. And they answered him, 'Wheresoever you go, we shall follow in your footsteps.'"

"On that day ignorance was conquered by the Incarnation, and the universe was given back its eagerness for its unparalleled development: on the day when Christ, to save the world that was withering away even in its natural roots, took his place at the head of creation."[30]

This love of Christ for creation is not, however, love "at a distance." The risen Jesus transcends all time and space by reason of his resurrected state, and so he can be fully present to every time and every space, to me now. He is present, through his love, loving me now.

Teilhard not only wrote this; he believed it and he lived it. His union in love with Jesus Christ risen, that Jesus Christ who is Lord of all (organically, not just juridically, present to everything holding it in existence by his love) was the centre of his life.

Official Jesuit censors often refused Teilhard's writings approval for publication partly or wholly because the censors held Teilhard's ideas pantheistic and therefore heretical. The censors argued this way: if Jesus Christ is present everywhere in the way that Pierre Teilhard de Chardin claimed he was, then everything is Jesus. Individual creatures cannot be differentiated from their

Creator present in Christ, and therefore all things are Jesus Christ; everything and everyone is God. The Jesuit censors did not and perhaps could not understand Teilhard's thought. They read him in the categories of Saint Thomas Aquinas and of the theology of their time, their own theology, and so they misread him.

In many places in his writings, Teilhard explains clearly the union of all things with Jesus Christ, and often he contrasts that union with the belief of pantheistic religions that hold all things to be one, and God. True union differentiates the elements united, and that differentiation takes place at the level of the union. For example, the organs of the human body are differentiated according to function. The five players on a basketball team are differentiated according to their team union; each one does something a little different, plays his own position. Members of a surgical team have different specialities, do diverse things in the operating room. Union differentiates.

The error of pantheistic systems, like some Eastern religions, lies here: they recognise, God, as more interior to creatures than the creatures are to themselves; and they conclude that therefore everything is God. Christianity has a doctrine of creation. The Creator makes creatures to be precisely not him but themselves; he gives them existence. Teilhard explains creation as creation in Christ; existence comes from Jesus risen holding creatures in existence by his love for them, in *a differentiating union that makes them to be not him but themselves.*

When true union exists between persons, at the level of persons, then the differentiation produced by the union takes the form of a *personalization*. The persons united in love are personalised, grow as persons because of the union. And this is true of our union with Jesus. Jesus unites me to himself in love. And that union is the main source of my personal growth. He creates me now, every day, every moment, through loving me.

The Lord of all who holds the world in existence, moving it forward by his love, holds me in his hand, in his heart, moves me forward, gives me life and growth.

A reading from Teilhard

Christ is the instrument, the centre, the term of *all* creation; by him, everything is created, sanctified, vivified. All things find their coherence in Christ. He is the first and he is the head. In him everything was begun and everything holds together and everything is consummated. He is the Alpha and the Omega, the beginning and the end, the foundation stone and the keystone. Jesus is he in whom all things are created and he in whom the entire world in all its depth, its length, its breadth, its grandeur, its physical and its spiritual, comes to be, takes on consistence. The world is above all a work of continuous creation in Christ. (Adapted from a series of short quotations, R. Faricy, *Teilhard de Chardin's Theology of the Christian in the World,* Sheed and Ward, New York, 1967, page 113.)

The universal influence of Jesus Christ, far from disassociating things, consolidates them; far from confusing things, it differentiates them. (Adapted from the essay, 'Mon univers', 1924, quoted in R. Faricy, *Teilhard de Chardin's Theology of the Christian in the World,* op.sit. page 119.)

Only union *through* love and *in* love (using the word "love" in its widest and most real sense of "mutual internal affinity") because it brings individuals together, not superficially and tangentially but centre to centre, can have the property of not merely differentiating but also personalising. (Adapted from *The Future of Man,* Collins, London, 1964, page 235.)

Prayerful considerations

We can find examples of personalising love all around us: the love of a married couple that truly love one another and sacrifice for one another does not lead the couple to form one amorphous blob. On the contrary, in that union of love, lived out every day, each grows as a person. Each becomes herself or himself. The same is true of the love of parents for their children; the children become themselves, their own persons, within that union of affirming love. Love creates us, makes us more ourselves, personalises us.

This is true, above of all, of union with Jesus. His love, accepted in me, received by me, helps me to be myself, to grow; it creates me more. The greatest saints have been the greatest persons and the greatest individuals. Francis of Assisi, so normal that many thought him foolish. Ignatius of Loyola, neurotic and with lots of psychological problems, but an outstanding person, close to Jesus. Catherine of Siena, forceful, strong, dynamic, and loving and tender, a great person made that way through her prayerful union with Jesus. This is true too of people close to the Lord and in our own century: Mother Teresa of Calcutta, Martin Luther King, and Pierre Teilhard de Chardin himself.

- All the world around me, all the universe is resplendent, luminous with Christ's love. All created things are held in being by love. How much more I myself to whom he says, "I am the Lord your God, the Holy One of Israel, your Saviour. I have given Egypt for your ransom, Cush and Seba in return for you. Since I regard you as precious, since you are honoured and I love you" (Is 43:4).

- Read Jesus' words to his disciples the evening that he was arrested, the night before his crucifixion, in John, chapter 15, verses 1 to 9. Concentrate on the phrases below in the first paragraph under "God's Word". Read slowly, and prayerfully. Then put the text aside and be with the Lord. Talk to him in your own words, or just be with him, remaining in his love.

- During the day repeat frequently the prayer, "Thank you, Jesus, for the gift of life; thank you for loving me." Or any short prayer that you make up.

God's Word

I am the true vine... I am the vine; you are the branches... Remain in my love (Jn 15:1-9).

In him were created all things in heaven and on earth: everything visible and everything invisible, thrones, ruling forces, sovereignties, powers – all things were created through him and for him. He exists before all things and in him all things hold together (Col 1:16-17).

Closing prayer: Jesus, you are everywhere, loving; and you are here present to me personally, loving me, renewing me in love. Teach me to turn to you. Give me the gift of an awareness of your loving presence to me, in my life. I ask you this, Jesus, in your own name. Amen.

14

Hope

The grace I ask: The spirituality of Pierre Teilhard de Chardin is for people living in the world today, a world conscious that it is headed into a future that it sees as uncertain and even threatening, at a collective level and sometimes at a personal level. The central mystery of Teilhard's spirituality is the ultimate future: the Second Coming of Jesus Christ, the Parousia. The central virtue of his spirituality is the virtue that helps us to move into the future, the virtue of hope. I ask for the grace of hope, born of a living faith in Jesus, Lord of all, my Lord.

Prayer: I hope in you, Jesus; teach me to hope in you. I trust in you, Jesus; teach me to trust in you.

Teilhard

In 1947, the Jesuit General had a Jesuit in Paris, to gather together a dossier of all Teilhard's so far unpublished writings; to submit it to him, to the General in Rome, for censorship. Teilhard, of course, had been censored and unfavourably judged for decades; but this was a last chance for approval from official censors and for consequent publication. Among the Jesuit censors: the holy and strong minded Frenchman Charles Boyer, the courageous and absolutely upright Belgian Edouard Dhanis, and the lion of pre-Vatican II Jesuit theologians, the man who had written the doctrine of the Mystical Body of Christ for Pope Pius XII, Sebastian Tromp. Outstanding theologians, they dominated Roman Catholic theology before the Second Vatican Council, they carried weight; if they considered Teilhard heretical, in the eyes of the Jesuit General they could not be wrong.

Teilhard, called to Rome by the General in October, 1948, received the verdict of the censors on his writings: negative. At best, his writings were dangerous. At worst, they were unorthodox, heretical, against the Catholic faith. He could not publish, he could not even accept any invitations to teach in Paris. Teilhard was crushed; all hope of publishing was gone forever. His real life's work, not his science but his religious thought, would never be seen, never be read. He left Rome shattered.

A few months later, a letter arrived for Teilhard in Paris from the Father General. The General said "no" to everything: no publications on matters touching on religion; Teilhard's two main books, *The Phenomenon of Man* and *The Divine Milieu,* could never be published; an invitation to give a series of lectures at Columbia University in New York was to be declined; all further public philosophical, religious, theological, or spiritual discussion on Teilhard's part was forbidden. There was no longer any hope.

"My General doesn't *want* to understand!" he exclaimed to a friend. To another friend, he wrote, "Those people in Rome are living on another planet!"[31]

Teilhard kept writing. His writings remained unpublished. He gave no talks on anything except science.

But he kept reflecting and he kept writing. He kept hoping in Jesus risen that somehow his writings and his ideas would sometime help people and help the Church. He kept hoping right up until his death on Easter Sunday, 1955, the feast of the resurrection, the celebration of hope. After his death, of course, his hopes came true.

A reading from Teilhard

Tomorrow? But who can really guarantee us a tomorrow? And without the assurance that there is a tomorrow, can we really go on living, we to whom has been given – perhaps for the first time in history – the terrible gift of looking ahead? Sickness of the dead-end – the anguish of feeling shut in. This time at last we have put our finger on the place where it hurts.

As I have said before, what makes the world we live in specifically modern is this: in the world and around it we have discovered Evolution. And let me now add something: what makes the modern world uneasy at its very roots is that it cannot be sure, and it does not see how it ever could be sure, that there is an outcome – *a suitable outcome* – to that evolution. *(Le phe'nomene humain,* Seuil, 1955, page 254.)

To the eyes of faith, instead of some vague centre of convergence envisaged as the ultimate end of this process of evolution, the personal and definite reality of Jesus Christ appears. (Adapted from *The Future of Man,* op.sit. page 34.)

In a world certainly open at its summit in Christ Jesus, we no longer risk dying of suffocation. *("Le Christique,"* quoted in R. Faricy, *Teilhard de Chardin's Theology of the Christian in the World,* op.sit. page 94.)

Prayerful considerations

There is a way out for the human species, for the world. The universe is not closed. Faith tells us that this world is headed toward a future focal point, the Second Coming of Christ. And that is the world's way out, its transformation in and through the end of the world into the world-to-come.

And there is an ultimately successful outcome promised to the life of each one of us, there is a way out. Jesus risen is the way. Just as he will come at the end of the world, so too he comes to each of us who believe and hope in him – he is with each of us now, and he will come to each of us at our death. There is hope for the world. There is hope for each of us; we hope in Jesus Christ.

He has not promised me that I will not suffer, that I will not have the cross in my life. On the contrary, if I want to be his disciple, I must take up my cross and follow him. But he does promise me that my life will have an ultimately successful outcome, in him.

- I could not care for myself more, or seek my own happiness more, than Jesus does. He sees the whole picture. I can put my trust in his love.

- Read the Twenty-third Psalm, below, slowly, taking a phrase or a line at a time, in the presence of the Lord and applying it to him, your Good Shepherd.

- Frequently during the day repeat the prayer, "Lord Jesus, I trust in you." Or make up a brief prayer of your own and say that often during the day.

God's Word

> You are my shepherd;
> I shall not want.
> In verdant pastures you give me repose.
> Beside restful waters you lead me;
> you refresh my soul.
> You guide me in right paths
> for your name's sake.
> Even though I walk in the dark valley
> I fear no evil;
> for you are at my side.
> Your rod and your staff give me courage.
> You spread the table before me
> in the sight of my foes.
> You anoint my head with oil;
> my cup brims over.
> Only goodness and kindness follow me
> all the days of my life;
> and I shall dwell in your house
> for years to come.

> Look, I am coming soon… I am the Alpha and the Omega, the First and the Last, the Beginning and the End (Rev 22:12-13).

Closing prayer: Lord Jesus Christ, you are Lord of all things and you are Lord of the future. You hold the future, my future, the future of those I love, the future of my country, the future of the world, in your hands. I do not know what the future holds, but I do know who holds it, hidden from me but clear to you. You hold the future in your hands. I put all my hope in you. I trust in you. You are my future. Amen.

15

The contemplation to gain love

The grace I ask: The theme of this last meditation is "thanksgiving," I ask for a thankful heart, for the thanksgiving that leads to greater appreciation of the gift and of the giver and so to a greater love of him.

Prayer: Lord Jesus, teach me to appreciate and to be grateful to you for your gifts around me, in my life.

Teilhard

The Spiritual Exercises of Ignatius Loyola that Pierre Teilhard de Chardin made every year for his annual retreat close with an exercise called "The contemplation to gain love." The exercise begins with a short consideration that love consists of deeds rather than words, and is expressed in gift giving. The exercise asks the retreatant to consider God's gifts, one by one. Then, to see how God is present in each gift, to consider his active working in each gift, and to understand that every gift comes from the transcendent goodness of God. At each one of these steps, the retreatant thanks God, and responds by a prayer of self-offering, by the gift of oneself to God.

Teilhard made this exercise every year at least once, but in his own way each time. His retreat notes are always sketchy when he comes to the last day. It seems clear that he did make the contemplation more as less as outlined by Ignatius, but in a Christ-centred way that understands all things as organically anchored in, rooted in and dependent on, Jesus Christ risen who draws all things to himself. Teilhard's prayer is not to God in general, nor to God the Father, but to Jesus Christ risen. And Teilhard finds Jesus everywhere, in all his gifts, in all creation, actively working, loving, animating, and drawing all things to himself.

We can see from Teilhard's retreat notes that on the last day of each annual retreat he prayed about and to the risen Christ present, active, giving, loving, in all of creation. "Your main purpose" he reflects, "in this revealing to us of your heart was to enable our love to escape from the constrictions of the too narrow, too precise, too limited image of you which we had fashioned for ourselves. What I discern in your breast is simply a furnace of fire; and the more I fix my gaze on its ardency the more it seems to me that all around it the contours of your body melt away and become enlarged beyond all measure, till the only features I can distinguish in you are those of the face of a world which has burst into flame."[32]

Teilhard made this prayer of the retreat following Ignatius Loyola's "Contemplation to gain love." In the notebook margin of the notes for the eighth and last day of his 1940 retreat in Beijing, China, he has the words, "Contemplation to gain love" – an excellent text and outline!"

He made the contemplation in his own way. In his

1943 retreat notes, he wrote: "The Contemplation to gain love: almost exactly right, and at the same time, not right. The organic dimension is missing." Teilhard, seeing Christ in all things, finds the missing dimension as he prays: "Glorious Lord Christ: the divine influence secretly diffused and active in the depths of matter, and the dazzling centre where all the innumerable fibres of the manifold meet; power as implacable as the world and as warm as life; you whose forehead is of the whiteness of snow, whose eyes are of fire, and whose feet are brighter than molten gold; you whose hands imprison the stars; you who are the first and the last, the living and the dead and the risen again; you who gather into your exuberant unity every beauty, every affinity, every energy, every mode of existence; it is you to whom my being cried out with a desire as vast as the universe, 'In truth your are my Lord and my God'."[33]

Teilhard made the Ignatian prayer exercise in such a way as to find Jesus risen truly and actively in his gifts, drawing all things to himself in the direction of his second coming and the beginning of the world to come.

A reading from Teilhard

> The greatest and most necessary attribute we could recognise in Jesus Christ risen is that of exerting a real and supreme influence on every cosmic reality without exception... Jesus would not be the God of Saint Paul, nor the God of my heart, if, face to face with the lowliest and most material creature, I could not say, "I cannot understand this thing, I cannot grasp it, I cannot be fully in contact with it, except in function of him who gives to the natural whole of which it is a part, its full reality and its final

determination."... "The universe is physically impregnated to the very marrow of its being by... his influence. The presence of the Incarnate Word penetrates everything as a universal element. It shines at the common heart of things as a centre that is infinitely intimate to them and at the same time (since it coincides with universal fulfilment) infinitely distant *(Science et Christ,* Seuil, 1965, pages 85-86).

What is important is not just to see the Lord revealed in all things, but to live that, to take his active presence seriously, to respond to it... It's not sufficient to understand the plans for the construction of an aeroplane; you have to build it and fly it! (Unpublished retreat notes, for the last day of Teilhard's 1950 retreat, dedicated to "The Contemplation to gain love.")

Prayerful considerations

You can make now, "The Contemplation to gain love," the same way that Teilhard made it in his annual retreats.

- Make two considerations. First, that love consists more of deeds than of words. Second, that love is expressed in gift giving, and that mutual love is characterised by exchange of gifts. Then prayerfully consider, one by one, some of the gifts that Jesus has given you or continues to give you, thanking him for each gift.

    For example: redemption through his death on the cross, for you personally as though you were the only other person besides him who walked on earth. Creation: that you exist, that the world exists with its beauty. Consider the gifts of life, of this day, of health, of friends, of family. Consider other gifts that come to mind, of people, or things, or situations, or events. In your own words, thank him for each of these gifts. This may take some time. Do not do it in a hurry.

Finally, consider what gift you in return can give to the Lord, and say slowly the prayer that Teilhard prayed several times at the end of every retreat, the prayer that Ignatius Loyola places at the end of his Spiritual Exercises.

> Take Lord, and receive all my liberty, my memory, my understanding, my entire will – all that I have and possess. You have given it all to me. To you, Lord, I return it. Everything is yours; do with it what you will. Give me your love and your grace. That is enough for me.

- Take each of the gifts that you looked at in the paragraph above, and consider that, Jesus, is in some way present in each of those gifts, holding them in existence, keeping them going. And that, he does the same for you, stays present in love in you and to you, keeps you in existence and acting. Thank him in your own words for the gift of himself in each of his gifts to you. Then repeat the prayer above, "Take, Lord, and receive…"

- Again, take each of the gifts you have been considering, and see how Jesus is in some way active in each one, working for you in each gift. Thank him in your own words for his activity in each gift. And repeat the "Take, Lord, and receive" prayer.

- Read slowly Psalm 138, below. Thank the Lord in the words of the psalm. And thank him for whatever gifts come to mind: creation, redemption, his love, his presence, your family, the weather, other people.

- During the day repeat the prayer, "Thank you, Jesus." Or make up your own short prayer, and say that often.

God's Word

I thank you, Lord, with all my heart;
I sing praise to you before the angels.
I worship at your holy temple and praise your name
because of your constant love and faithfulness,
because you have shown that you and your word are exalted.
You answered me when I called to you;
you built up strength within me...
Even though you are exalted,
you care for the lowly.
The proud cannot hide from you.
Even when I am surrounded by troubles,
you keep me safe...
Your faithful love endures forever.
Complete the work that you have begun (Ps 138).

Closing prayer: Lord Jesus, thank you for everything. Thank you for my existence, for the gift of life. Thank you because you died for me on the cross by name, as though I were the only other person besides you to ever walk on the earth; and you would do it again to save me if you had to. Thank you for my personal vocation, to be this person in the situation in the world that I find myself in. Thank you for the people in my life that I love, and for those who love me. Thank you for today. Thank you for the gift of prayer. Thank you for the gift of your love, and for the gift of yourself.

Lord, you not only give me gifts, but you yourself are in the gifts, working, and working things out, for me. Thank you. Amen.

Notes

1. George Gaylord Simpson, 'Studies in the Earliest Primates,' *Bulletin of the American Museum of Natural History,* Vol. LXXXVII, Art. IV, pp. 185-212, New York, July 31, 1940.
2. 'The Heart of Matter' in *The Heart of Matter,* Collins, Lon don, and Harper & Row, New York, 1964, p. 46.
3. 'Letters from a Soldier Priest,' *The Making of a Mind,* Collins, London, and Harper & Row, New York, 1965, pp. 47-48.
4. 'Christ in the World of Matter,' *Hymn of the Universe,* Collins, London, and Harper & Row, New York, 1965, pp. 39-51.
5. *Letters to Le'ontine Zanta,* Collins, London, 1969, p. 71.
6. 'The Heart of Christ in the Spirituality of Teilhard de Chardin,' Robert Faricy, *Gregorianum,* Rome, Vol. 69, 2 (1988) p. 268.
7. *Writings in Time of War,* Collins, London, 1968, pp. 205-224.
8. *Hymn of the Universe,* op.sit. pp. 19-37.
9. *Hymn of the Universe,* op. sit. pp. 17 and 19.
10. Both letters quoted in R. Faricy, *All Things in Christ,* Collins, Font Paperbacks, London, 1981, p. 88.
11. Quoted in *Letters to Le'ontine Zanta,* op.sit. p. 30.
12. 'Letter to Valensin', quoted by R. D'Ouince, 'L'obeissance dans la vie du Pere Teilhard de Chardin,' *L'homme devant Dieu,* Aubier, 1964, Vol. III, p. 336.
13. Quoted in *Letters to Le'ontine Zanta,* op.sit. p. 33.

14. *The Letters of Teilhard de Chardin and Lucille Swan,* ed. T. King and M. W. Gilbert, Georgetown U. Press, Washington D.C., 1993, p. 243.
15. 'Letter to Valensin,' d'Ouince, op.sit. p. 343.
16. *The Phenomenon of Man,* Collins, London, and Harper & Brothers, NewYork, 1959, p. 312.
17. 'Operative Faith', *Writings in Time of War,* op.sit. p. 230.
18. *Journal,* p. 337.
19. These and the following quotations from Teilhard's unpublished notes are taken from R. Faricy, 'Teilhard de Chardin's Spirituality of the Cross' *Horizons,* vol. 3, 1976, pp. 14-15.
20. R. Faricy, *Gregorianum,* op.sit.
21. Quoted in M. and E. Lukas, *Teilhard,* Collins, London, and Harper & Row, 1966, p. 243.
22. R. Faricy, *Gregorianum,* op.sit.
23. Quoted in R. Speaight, *Teilhard de Chardin,* Collins, London, 1967, p. 331.
24. Adapted from a quotation in Thomas King, 'The Milieux Teilhard Left Behind,' in *America,* March 30, 1985, p. 253.
25. Unpublished retreat notes, 1940, eighth day: the Kingdom.
26. Adapted from *The Making of a Mind,* op.sit. pp. 246-247.
27. *Genese d'une pense'e,* pp. 191-192.
28. *Le milieu divin,* Seuil, 1957, p. 168
29. 'Cosmic Life,' *Writings in Time of War,* op.sit. p. 59.
30. *Writings in Time of War* op.sit. pp. 171-202.
31. 'The Struggle Against the Multitude,' *Writings in Time of War,* op.sit. pp. 106-107.
32. Lukas, *Teilhard,* op.sit. p. 274.
33. 'The Mass on the World', *Hymn of the Universe,* op.sit. p. 34.